Praise for
For Young Men Only

"Turn off your iPod and cell phone, grab this book, and delve into the secret thoughts of hundreds of young women boiled down into eight simple, fresh chapters. Trust me, you won't be disappointed."

—COLIN CREEL, author of *Crossroads: Navigating your Calling and Career* and *Perspectives: A Spiritual Life Guide for Twentysomethings*

"*For Young Men Only* is for any guy who has thought *Is it just me?* when it comes to relating to girls. Jeff and Eric slice through the beautiful and elaborate female mind and lay down a path that is clear and direct."

—DR. JOE WHITE, president of Kanakuk Kamps

"When you buy something electronic, it always includes a user's guide. Sometimes you read it; sometimes you don't. This book is a user's guide for teen guys as they learn how to relate to girls. Jeff and Eric have covered almost everything you need to know. And they've done it in a way that's really easy to follow. I think you ought to read it."

—DR. ROBERT WOLGEMUTH, best-selling author of *The Most Important Year in a Man's Life* and *Dad's Bible*

"Two thumbs up for *FYMO*! It's a great read for *every* young man— including the ones who are certain they already know everything about women. Maybe it should be required reading. Good job, Jeff and Eric."

—KENDRA SMILEY, conference speaker and author
of *Do Your Kids a Favor...Love Your Spouse*

"Funny, helpful, simple—just the way guys like it."

—CHAD EASTHAM, author of *The Truth About Guys*

"Finally a book for guys about all things girl! Jeff and Eric have revealed the truth about what those 'aliens' really want and need from us guys. And they do so by giving young men a unique glimpse into the minds and hearts of girls. Get ready, guys. On the following pages you'll learn more than you could imagine about what girls really think—and why."

—JEFFREY DEAN, founder of Jeffrey Dean Ministries
and author of *Watch This* and *This is Me*

"Jeff and Eric's hilarious sense of humor makes this book a fast and entertaining read. Even though *FYMO* is based on a huge survey, it's not just facts and percentages. The authors get to the real heartbeat of who we are as girls and what makes us tick."

—LIZ, high-school girl

"I am so glad you're telling guys this stuff. That means maybe I won't have to! Could you give a copy to every guy at my high school?"

—CAMI, high-school girl

jeff feldhahn & eric rice
with shaunti feldhahn

from the authors of the bestselling *for men only*

for young men only

a guy's guide
to the
alien gender

MULTNOMAH
BOOKS

FOR YOUNG MEN ONLY
PUBLISHED BY MULTNOMAH BOOKS
12265 Oracle Boulevard, Suite 200
Colorado Springs, Colorado 80921
A division of Random House Inc.

ISBN 978-1-60142-020-6

Published in association with the literary agency of Calvin W. Edwards, 1220 Austin Glen Drive, Atlanta, GA 30338.

Published in the United States by WaterBrook Multnomah, an imprint of The Doubleday Publishing Group, a division of Random House Inc., New York.

MULTNOMAH and its mountain colophon are registered trademarks of Random House Inc.

Library of Congress Cataloging-in-Publication Data
Feldhahn, Jeff.
    For young men only : a guy's guide to the alien gender / Jeff Feldhahn and Eric Rice. — 1st ed.
        p. cm.
    ISBN 978-1-60142-020-6
    1. Teenage boys—Religious life. 2. Teenage boys—Conduct of life. 3. Man-woman relationships—Religious aspects—Christianity. I. Rice, Eric. II. Title.
    BV4541.3.F45 2008
    248.8'32—dc22

                                  2008021400

Printed in the United States of America
2008—First Edition

10 9 8 7 6 5 4 3 2 1

From Jeff:
To Bill and Roberta Feldhahn,
who survived the raising of four boys
with their humor, sanity, and marriage intact.

———

From Eric:
To Paul and Melba Rice, married fifty-three years.
They laughed and loved to the fullest.

A Preface for Grownups
Who Are Peeking In

To the grownups who are worriedly sneaking a peek (Mom, Dad, youth leader...you know who you are): we're glad you're peeking! As parents ourselves, we affirm you as the most important guardians of your teens, including where they get information and advice. And when it has to do with the opposite sex, we "extra affirm" your concern!

We wrote *For Young Men Only* for a teen you care about—a young man-in-the-making who spends hours wondering what girls are like, what they think, what they want. Too often he simply doesn't know, or else his answers come from all the wrong places. Our goal has been to deliver an eyeopening book that draws on solid research to help teen guys understand and honor the unique way girls are wired. Many adult readers of *For Men Only* and *For Women Only* (previous books in the series) have told us, "I wish I had learned these truths *before* I got married." That's why we're confident this book can help your teen enjoy dramatically healthier and happier relationships in the future.

As you review the pages ahead, keep a few things in mind:

▸ We've taken some risks to present our findings in a way that meets guys right where they are. Some in our audience will be church kids and some won't. Regardless, we look at each issue from their perspective and felt needs *first*. Then we make sure they see and understand what they've been missing or never knew.

▸ This is a book about how girls think. It's not a dating advice book (although we recommend a few tips as we go along). What your teen reads here is intended to help him whether he is in a relationship or not. We assume that our reader at least has an interest in getting to know or understand girls, even just as friends. That natural interest is our starting point for showing him how he can support, honor, and protect girls, now and for the rest of his life.

▸ Much of what is here will surprise your teen—maybe you, too—so we encourage you to use this book as a conversation starter. God has granted you influence in your teen boy's life for a very good reason.

In a world that seems to conspire against families who care about honoring others in relationships, we pray you'll find *For Young Men Only* just the resource you've been looking for!

Warmly,

Jeff & Shaunti Feldhahn and Eric & Lisa Rice

Contents

WHAT MOST GUYS NEVER KNOW

To find the truth, we take you to the ultimate source—more than one thousand of them

There are so many reasons why you don't need this book. You don't need it to know how to text a girl in the middle of a roller-coaster ride. Or to build a computer on your bedroom floor. Or to belch the alphabet in tune, or kill a city full of zombies with just your thumbs, or sink your famous no-look jump shot.

All that you can already do.

And for all those reasons you are already...legend.

On the other hand, like most young males, you live among aliens who don't know or appreciate your achievements. The aliens, of course, are girls. Some of them, especially the cute ones, have the power to make you stutter, shake, and fall on your behind right when you want to look your coolest.

You know it's true. Girls drive us crazy. They can turn a famous jump shot into nothing but air. They can make us so confused we want to scream.

So we have to ask, will you—male legend—survive girls with your coolness intact?

Plenty of guys don't. We know. Well, at least I (Eric) know. When I was a teen, I drove all the way from Texas to Tennessee on a hot day just to hear a girl say, "Bye, Eric." Very hot, very bad day.

All that stuff about stutter, shake, and fall down? That was me. Most of what I learned about girls was from urban legends or in locker rooms or by guesswork. And most of what I learned was dead wrong. That's why we decided to write *FYMO,* which is code for *For Young Men Only: A Guy's Guide to the Alien Gender.*

Now that we're post-cool but also post-stuttering grownups, we want to help teen guys understand, talk to, listen to, get to know, learn from, care for, enjoy...maybe even *impress* a girl. Sure, it's not quite as lofty a goal as stopping terrorism or bringing back the glaciers. But it's something smart guys care about—and smart girls too. Understanding how girls think can make a huge difference in your happiness now and in the future. Even better, a crash course in Girl 101 can put you way ahead of most other guys, who will spend the rest of their lives being totally confused.

In the book you're holding, enlightenment starts with you. You bring your legendary genius. We bring our shocking data. Pretty soon you can get inside her head.

A crash course in Girl 101 can put you way ahead of most other guys.

"No Way!"

Yes, *FYMO* takes you inside a teen girl's head (scary but fascinating, you have to admit). We help you accomplish that feat by listening to hundreds of smart, likable girls who were willing to talk about themselves—and keep it honest. (And if you think we hunted down only boring, shallow, or unappealing girls for this project, jump to www.foryoungmenonly.com. You'll get a different picture.)

How are we able to deliver insights that will get you shouting "No way!" and change how you think forever?

Let me (Jeff) explain. Shaunti, my wife, just happens to be a Harvard-trained policy analyst who unexpectedly became a social researcher. One day she woke up to the fact that men really do think differently than women. (Okay, sometimes we don't think at all, but let's not go there.) Shaunti realized that even though she loved someone as smooth as me, she simply didn't "get" a lot about me. Not just didn't get. More like had no clue.

And here's the weirdest part: I had no clue that she had no clue.

When Shaunti asked around, she discovered that our problem was a common one. In fact, she talked to men and women from all over who had simply given up on thinking that you *could* understand someone of the opposite sex, even one you loved very much.

That realization prompted her to launch a research project that asked men how they really felt about certain topics. Especially about some of the more hidden, difficult, and important aspects of being a man. Their answers led Shaunti to write *For Women Only: What You Need to Know About the Inner Lives of Men*.

It became a national bestseller. Men everywhere breathed a sigh of relief because suddenly they weren't treated like freaks. And women everywhere realized they could know and love their man for who he really was, not for who they thought he was. We're still amazed at how often just one new insight about the opposite sex can turn a light bulb on over our heads—and turn a relationship completely around.

Other bestsellers in the series followed, including *For Men Only* and *For Young Women Only*. Each of them uses a carefully designed, nationally representative scientific survey to help one gender understand what goes on inside the heads of the other.

Which brings us to *FYMO*.

Honestly, we delayed bringing out this installment in the series as long as possible. Would your average teen guy read a book about how girls think? Watch a YouTube clip maybe. Or wait for the manga version. But actually read a carefully researched book about how to figure out and relate to girls? We weren't sure.

At first it was just worried parents and about a million teen girls who asked us to write this book. Parents said things like, "Our darling son seems somewhat, oh, challenged around the opposite, you know, s-s-sex." Girls said things like, "Boys are just stupid."

Then teen guys themselves started asking. After the hundredth high schooler told us he wished there were a "chick manual" for ordinary guys, we decided to go for it.

> Parents said things like, "Our darling son seems somewhat, oh, challenged around the opposite, you know, s-s-sex." Girls said things like, "Boys are just stupid."

Our No-Rehash Promise

Shaunti and I (Jeff) enlisted my best buddy, Eric Rice (the husband of Lisa, Shaunti's coauthor on *For Young Women Only*), to help me write this book. Being a talented screenwriter and director, Eric makes the perfect coauthor for this narrative. Also, he's father to three of the smartest, most attractive teen girls we know. Also, he's insane. (Maybe it's the teenage daughters.)

To make sure we were asking the right questions, Eric and I started with some things we never understood about girls when we were in high school. Then we set up focus groups with dozens of Atlanta-area teenage girls. With Lisa and Shaunti helping to host the groups (so the girls felt they could talk safely and candidly), we started to identify important problem areas to cover.

Interesting questions came naturally to our team. Lisa is a journalist, Shaunti is a relationship analyst, I'm a lawyer, and Eric is crazy.

To every potential topic we applied one important test: would it be a big surprise for today's teenage guys? If not, we weren't interested. We didn't want to rehash the obvious stuff. We didn't want to preach. We just wanted to go for those shockers that most guys wouldn't believe—but that were true...and were true for most girls, no matter their ethnic or religious backgrounds, no matter where they live or what kind of cars their families drive.

Next, Shaunti and Lisa hit the malls around Atlanta to ask questions of hundreds of teens. And since they regularly travel and speak around the country, they also randomly interviewed any teenage girls they came across ("So, Courtney, what would you be thinking if a guy said *this*...?").

Finally, we took what we were hearing informally and tested it with an expensive, scientific, nationally representative survey of more than four hundred girls, conducted by the highly regarded firm Decision Analyst. If we were going to claim that girls really did think a certain way, then an official, expensive national survey had to confirm it. (Did we mention it was expensive?)

After we analyzed the survey results, we boiled down all the subjects on which most girls agreed and came up with these six lightbulb-over-the-head insights.

We didn't want to rehash the obvious stuff. We just wanted to go for those shockers that most guys wouldn't believe—but that were true.

	Six Big Surprises	
Chapter	*What most guys think*	*The surprise*
2 Abercrombie Boy vs. Our Hero, Average Joe *Why ordinary guys have a real chance with great girls*	*The best girls always go for guys who are rich and ripped.*	A girl is most attracted to a guy's hidden qualities.
3 Why Good Girls Like Bad Boys *Understanding a girl's greatest secret fear— and what you can do about it*	*Girls have this weird attraction to "bad guys" who come on strong, then usually treat them like junk.*	A girl is secretly afraid she's not special or attractive, so she'll be drawn to a guy who affirms her by pursuing her.
4 When Girls Stop Making Sense *A code breaker's guide to baffling female behavior*	*When girls get emotional and irrational, guys are out of luck. There's nothing a guy can do but run.*	When a girl gets emotional, she's probably not irrational—and there's a lot a guy can do.
5 Breaking Up, Breaking You *Why girls go from "love" to "get lost" so fast—and how to keep from getting crushed*	*Girlfriends are heartless. When they want to break up, they send confusing messages, then dump the guy with no warning.*	Some girlfriends are heartless, sure, but mostly guys are clueless. Once you learn to read the signs, you can protect your heart— and maybe even win her back.

Six Big Surprises		
Chapter	*What most guys think*	*The surprise*
6 No Dropped Calls *How to talk and listen to a girl without looking like an idiot*	*Guys never know what to say to a girl, so they end up looking like idiots.*	A girl wants a guy to talk to her. But to really make an impression with her, a guy just needs to listen.
7 What It Really Means to Score *The truth about girls, guys, and sex*	*Girls want sex as much as guys do— and the way to score with her is to go all the way.*	A girl has hormones too, but she deeply hopes her guy won't press for sex. The way to really score with her is to be her protector.

And that's how this journey into the adolescent female brain came to be. In the end, more than one thousand girls provided input for this book. What we're bringing you, therefore, is not our opinion. (In some cases the research directly contradicted our opinion!) Instead, what we're bringing you are the heartfelt thoughts of the girls themselves.

Read This or You'll Explode

Before you begin your quest through the rest of the book, note these important points:

- *FYMO* was written weird but well. Eric and I wrote it with a lot of help from Shaunti and Lisa and some more help from our impossible-to-please editor, David Kopp. When you read "we" in this book, usually it means Jeff and Eric. But sometimes it means all long-suffering males (that would include you). When you read "I (Eric)" or "I (Jeff)," don't get alarmed. You don't have an author with multiple personality disorder. It just means one of us doesn't want the other guy to get credit for the amazing insight or funny story that follows.

- We're focusing only on what you need to know about girls but probably don't. We don't deal at all with what girls should know about you or other young male humanoids. If you want to find that out, sneak off with your girlfriend's copy of *For Young Women Only.*

- We present our survey results with confidence. But when we report that "most girls" think a certain way, remember that *most* means "most," not "all." There are exceptions to every rule, and you probably know one. To read the entire survey, go to www.foryoungmenonly.com.

- Our survey describes what girls *say* they think or want when it comes to guys, not what we believe they *should* think or want. We sometimes found ourselves wishing the truth were different. But that's the point of this book: the truth about how girls really think. Even when it's surprising or hard to hear.

‣ We approach life as Christians. This book describes what is going on inside teenage girls regardless of race, culture, or religion, and it outlines *their* advice for what guys can do to best relate to them. But in the parts of the book where *we* give advice, our convictions (like "the Bible is right") are just going to leak out. We hope you understand.

‣ We believe that learning how girls think is pretty important for both now and the future, regardless of whether you're dating right now or just want to be friends with the girls around you. There are many great books out there that pull together good biblical guidelines for dating, for example, but that isn't what we're doing here. *FYMO* is a short book, and in our limited space, our only focus is the honest truth about how girls are wired and how you can apply that in your life. (You can find pointers to other great resources at www.foryoungmenonly.com. You might start with *Boy Meets Girl* and other Joshua Harris books.)

‣ To help you and your friends get even more out of the book, we've included a short small-group discussion guide at the back of this book.

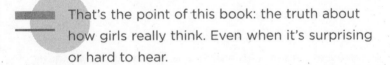

That's the point of this book: the truth about how girls really think. Even when it's surprising or hard to hear.

Confidence: The New Superpower

You may not realize it yet, but for the price of this book, we are handing you a silver platter of wisdom that will help you navigate the challenges of the alien gender with confidence—the confidence that comes from realizing that you actually understand what is going on around you. You will come away with a whole arsenal of new insights. You will move from the average "I don't really get girls" guy to someone with superpowers. You will basically have a master's degree in Girl.

We challenge you to use these powers wisely and not for your own selfish purposes. If we hear that you haven't used your new knowledge well, we will hunt you down and force you to sit through our twelve-hour, two-on-one seminar. And we'll charge you for it.

You ready for the adventure? Sit back for a fun ride and plenty of big—and amazingly helpful—surprises about how girls think. When you're done, be sure to let us know what happened.

> If we hear that you haven't used your new knowledge well, we will hunt you down and force you to sit through our twelve-hour, two-on-one seminar. And we'll charge you for it.

—Jeff & Eric (Shaunti & Lisa too)
www.foryoungmenonly.com

ABERCROMBIE BOY VS. OUR HERO, AVERAGE JOE

Why ordinary guys have a real chance with great girls

(Jeff) was sixteen years old, working at a restaurant, when my boss dared me to ask out the amazingly cute seventeen-year-old waitress. If she accepted, I would go home early with full pay. If she told me to get lost, I would work the rest of the day without pay.

Her name was Diane, and she was way out of my league. She was the head cheerleader and the favorite for homecoming queen at a rival high school. With quite a few of the employees watching, I had to walk into the break room and ask her out.

Heart hammering, I stepped up to the table where Diane sat. (Just so you know, I had never been on a date.) Trying not to shake or spontaneously combust, I swallowed hard, then gasped, "So, ah, would you like to go to a movie sometime?"

I couldn't think of what to do next, so I just stood there. Hours passed.

Then I heard her say, "That sounds like fun, Jeff. Okay!"

I started to breathe again. "Great!" I exclaimed. "How 'bout Saturday night?"

When she agreed, the deal was sealed.

That Saturday I went out on my very first date—with a beautiful girl. To top off a great evening, a bunch of my buddies saw me with Diane. My Big Dog ranking soared. But the evening wasn't over.

When I dropped Diane off at her home, I asked her if she'd had a good time.

She said, "Yes, I did. Thanks."

So, gathering my courage once again, I asked her if she'd like to go out again.

"Yeah, I think so," she said.

We said good-bye, and I probably patted her on the shoulder or something like that since I was too afraid to kiss her. And I drove away—crushed.

"Crushed?" you ask.

Yep. After all, she'd said, "Yeah, *I think so.*" I forgot about the "yeah" part and obsessed on the "I think so."

A familiar voice in my head started beating me up. *You were insane to think a girl like her would ever go out with you a second time. She can have any guy she wants. Protect yourself, Jeff. Don't put yourself out there for rejection.*

So I didn't ask her out again. Soon she quit working at that restaurant. We crossed paths at various times, and she was always sweet to me. But I could never get over my belief that I simply wasn't in her league and she wouldn't go out with me again.

I didn't learn until the following spring, when I was talking with Diane's best friend, that Diane had been puzzled and a little hurt when I never asked her out again. And by this time she was dating another guy. (Nicely done, Jeff.)

I eventually married a beautiful and amazing girl—also out of my league—who has been my wife for the past fourteen years. But I still carried around a bunch of misconceptions about how females are wired—completely wrong ideas that actually lasted until the research for these books blew them away.

So in this chapter we tackle one of those subjects most guys misunderstand, that brutal competition you probably know all about. We call the battle Abercrombie Boy vs. Our Hero, Average Joe. Your world—at school, on MySpace, in the media—seems overrun with perfectly dressed, seriously ripped guys who are dripping with money. You, on the other hand, probably don't see yourself as that guy. You're just you. Unfortunately, the girls who interest you, especially the more attractive and popular ones, seem to worship at Abercrombie Boy's feet.

Do you stand a chance?

Should you take the dare? Or keep to what you know you do well—rolling up higher and higher scores with your thumbs? And by the way, what *is* actually going on inside a girl's head when the guy who is standing in front of her is not 'Crombie Boy...but you?

Okay, you might be saying to yourself, *whatever you do, Jeff and Eric, don't give me false hope. Don't set me up to have my heart pulled out of my chest and stomped on in front of the world.*

Listen, there *is* hope. We know the truth. We are keepers of the Secret Fire. Read on…

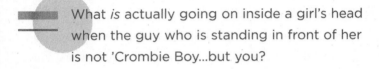

What *is* actually going on inside a girl's head when the guy who is standing in front of her is not 'Crombie Boy…but you?

Why Ordinary Guys Have Hope

In this chapter we're going to reveal one of the most shocking discoveries we made while working on this book: there's a high chance that the girls around you, including the ones you think are hardest to get, aren't looking for perfect Abercrombie Boy. What they really prefer is a guy who has other qualities that are more important to them.

We can almost hear you thinking, *Yeah, right.*

We understand. We've all been slumped in the cheap seats while that perfect cheerleader babe strolled by on the arm of the perfect guy. We think, *If she goes for him, there's no way she'd go for me.* Or we assume that the "perfect" guy is what all girls want.

Turns out we're wrong. And what's right is very good news. To help you grab hold of this amazing fact most guys miss, we've come up with what we call Four Crazy Truths. The first one is the hardest to believe.

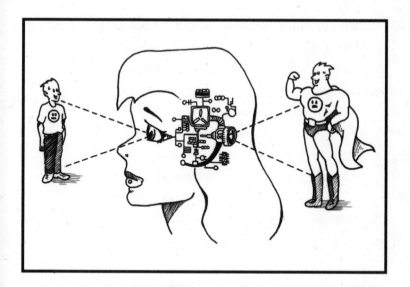

The Weird Wiring of the Female Eyeball

Sure, girls appreciate a good-looking guy. Humans are made that way. (Other life forms with eyeballs are too.) But our research for *FYMO* sheds light on something you may have only vaguely understood before: most girls just aren't wired to respond as visually as guys are. Instead, a girl's appreciation of a guy's looks is only part of what her brain considers about him. And, it turns out, it's not even the most important part. Which leads us to Crazy Truth 1.

Crazy Truth 1

Unlike a guy, a girl instinctively looks beyond looks.

When it comes to the guys who girls want to be in a relationship with, girls nearly always rank other qualities as more important than outward looks—and they mean it! Listen to how a few girls explained it:

▸ "Initial attractiveness is just not as important to a girl."

▸ "Actually, a guy gets more attractive when we see the great guy he really is."

▸ "Just because a girl sees an attractive guy and goes, 'He's so hot,' doesn't mean she wants to date him."

Those answers and others like them from hundreds of girls came in response to this question:

SURVEY Suppose you had a choice to go out with one of two guys at school who you don't know very well—Guy A or Guy B. Guy A is so good looking that he could be a magazine model, and he is captain of the football team, but you have heard through the grapevine that "he thinks he's all that." Guy B is only average looking, but you have heard through the grapevine that he's a nice guy who has a funny sense of humor. Both seem to have quite a few friends, and both are interested in going out with you, but you have to choose only one and not the other. Which one do you choose? (Choose one.)

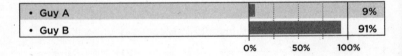

• Guy A	9%
• Guy B	91%

0%   50%   100%

Nine out of ten girls said they would choose Guy B! Huh? Still in disbelief, we upped the stakes a bit and asked the question another way:

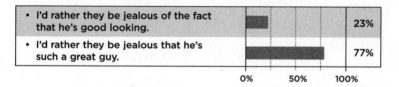

SURVEY If you secretly want your friends to be jealous about a guy you've caught, would you rather they be jealous that he's a good-looking guy or just a great guy? (Choose one.)

• I'd rather they be jealous of the fact that he's good looking.	23%
• I'd rather they be jealous that he's such a great guy.	77%

0%   50%   100%

This question took the truth about how girls are wired even further. We could summarize what we found like this: though we guys probably want our buddies to be envious that we have a hot babe on our arm, most girls think differently. Three out of four girls care so much about a guy's other qualities that *those* are the things they'd want their friends to be jealous of.

If you're reeling a bit, you're not alone. While doing the research, we had to constantly fight our own disbelief at what we were hearing. We had long, deep conversations that went like this.

Jeff: "Eric, are you believing this?"

Eric: "No way, bro. Can't be true, or I'm a dummy now and have been a dummy for a long time!"

Jeff: "Umm…"

Eric: "Let's go get a burger."

The truth about how girls see guys goes against so many male assumptions. That's why most of us need to change how we think about girls. Otherwise we'll be clueless when it comes to girls. And clueless doesn't look good on a man.

> "Just because a girl sees an attractive guy and goes, 'He's so hot,' doesn't mean she wants to date him."

Seeing Through to What's Inside

Still struggling to wrap your male video-cam brain around how girls see? There's more. Look at these comments:

- "Looks are not even on the radar screen for me. It is totally who he is on the inside."

- "Looks come and go, but you can't have a relationship on that. Eventually you have to live with someone. So you'd better find someone you like on the inside."

- "Real guys are attractive because of who they are inside. Besides, a hot guy without much personality quickly gets boring."

Truth 1 leads us to ask an important question: "So what are those other qualities that girls like so much?" Time to tackle Crazy Truth 2.

Crazy Truth 2

Inner qualities can make Average Joe more attractive than Abercrombie Boy.

When a girl says "other" qualities, she's not talking about money, popularity, his fine ride, or his taste in fashion. She means something deeper, something more personal. We wanted to know, so we asked.

SURVEY Which traits do you find most attractive in a guy?
Please rank these in order of your preference from
1 to 12, with 1 being best:

____ self-confident (without being arrogant) / willing to be unique / edgy

____ sense of humor / makes me laugh

____ adventuresome / spontaneous / unpredictable / fun / carefree attitude / risk taker

____ gentlemanly / thoughtful / considerate but not clingy / protective

____ good conversationalist with you and others / socially adept / not painfully shy

____ cocky / rule breaker

____ a genuine faith that influences his life

____ goal oriented / motivated

____ buff body

____ attractive face

____ rich

____ athletic

Before we give you the results, what do you guess the girls' top three answers are? Most guys guess "rich," "buff body," and "athletic," with a dash of "cocky" thrown in. After all, these are the qualities we'd kill to have more of, right?

Well, the girls in our survey picked three totally different answers. The top three traits that mattered most to girls were (1) "sense of humor," (2) "thoughtfulness," and (3) "self-confidence."

After that came "good conversationalist," "adventuresome," "goal oriented," "attractive face," and "genuine faith." And finally, at the very bottom of hundreds of girls' lists, came (9) "buff body," (10) "athletic," (11) "rich," and (12) "cocky."

At first we thought a virus had corrupted the data. I mean, ever watch TV or go to the movies? The girls always go for the buff, rich guy!

Well, amigo, the facts don't lie. And they come down strongly in favor of average guys. So if you're spending all your time at the gym or plotting ways to get rich quick, consider the fact that most girls aren't noticing those things as much as we thought they did.

The really good news is that what matters more to girls are qualities you don't have to be born with (unlike good looks or athletic ability). A sense of humor, a love of adventure, thoughtfulness, confidence—these are qualities that any motivated guy can learn with a little effort. (More about that later.)

Look at this comment from a girl who described how inner qualities make a guy attractive: "My boyfriend and I have been dating a year, but at first I thought he wasn't all that attractive. Then I got to know him. I saw that he was funny, thoughtful, and kind. Now he's one of the most attractive guys in the world."

"At first I thought he wasn't all that attractive. Then I got to know him. Now he's one of the most attractive guys in the world."

What Most Girls Really Want Most

First, let's take a closer look at the top three traits.

1. Sense of humor

Almost all the girls we interviewed talked about how important it is for guys to have a sense of humor. You may be thinking, *Well, I'm just not the class clown.* But that's not what the girls mean. Instead, they simply enjoy guys who enjoy life and sometimes make them laugh. Here's what we heard:

- "Life can be hard, and girls need guys who will help them look at life through a lighter, more humorous lens. It's okay to be serious, but sometimes we have a tendency to be too serious, and it's nice to have someone who will help us lighten up!"
- "When I see a guy with a sense of humor, I know he's lighthearted and doesn't take everything too seriously. I know he can find humor in everyday situations. That's really attractive."

2. Thoughtfulness

It's no surprise that a girl wants to feel special. But most guys assume that a girl gets that feeling by having somebody handsome, popular, or rich to be with. Come to find out, girls are looking for something else: a gentleman. (Caught you off guard, didn't it? Us too.)

The girls we surveyed said they feel most special when the guy they are with is considerate and well mannered. Not slimy smooth, mind you. Or putting on some act so she'll let you make out with her. But thoughtful and respectful in the little things. Look at how one girl put it:

> I see thoughtfulness as looking out for the other person's
> interests over your own. Tuning in to what they're thinking
> and needing and going through. Like if a guy notices that
> she's always frustrated when she mentions her after-school
> job, and he takes a few extra minutes to ask why. When a
> guy does something like that, you feel like a million bucks.

Being thoughtful should be a no-brainer since it's how most of us want to be treated. Yet average guys miss it all the time. Maybe because we're too self-conscious to notice the little stuff.

3. Self-confidence

Girls overwhelmingly like guys who seem to have a sense of confidence. As one girl put it, "A guy with average looks who has confidence is far more attractive to me than some model type who doesn't."

Just don't confuse self-confidence with conceit or cockiness. Most girls don't. They see right through the attitude that's hiding a poser. "Confidence in a guy is always appealing," one girl told us. "I don't mean trying so hard he just comes off as arrogant and cocky. That's a huge turnoff."

> "A guy with average looks who has confidence is far more attractive to me than some model type who doesn't."

Two More Things That Put You on Her Radar Screen

We want to mention two more inner qualities that came up all the time in our surveys—qualities that many girls put in or near the top three. (It seems girls can spot inner qualities like we can spot a Ferrari in a parking lot.)

1. Fun to be with + loves adventure

Over and over, girls told us things like, "We want to be with someone fun," and, "I don't want to talk to a puddle. I want to converse with someone who's fun." On the survey, we grouped these responses under one long heading: "adventuresome / spontaneous / unpredictable / fun / carefree attitude / risk taker."

That makes sense. Any guy wants to be these things. And at times we all struggle with frustration, anxiety, or uncertainty. Fun makes us forget all that for a moment and pulls us back to the bright side.

But we stumbled onto something very important: girls admitted to being bored a lot and to dreaming about being swept away on an adventure. The cool thing is, with a little advance thought, any guy can fill that role. You don't have to plan something official. Just let yourself enjoy life day to day, and bring her in on it ("Hey, let's go explore somewhere!").

And the fun doesn't have to be a big deal either. Powerful impressions are often made by the simplest acts. As one girl suggested, "Give her a flower just because it's Wednesday."

Look at how another girl put it: "Even if a guy just makes a joke now and then, it can turn a boring chem lab into a class a girl looks forward to. Because he's there."

2. Has a genuine faith

Faith didn't rank high for everyone, but for girls who identified themselves as having an important personal faith, it ranked *very* high.

We know a lot of guys who have personal beliefs they really care about, but they try to keep those beliefs out of sight, suspecting that most girls think anyone with "religious convictions" is boring or weird. Not so. In our survey, almost half of the girls who went to church or synagogue each week put this trait in their top three.

Now let's return to the land of Abercrombie Boy, where the news is *not* good for him. What we discovered next leads to another Crazy Truth you need to know.

Girls admitted to being bored a lot and to dreaming about being swept away on an adventure. The cool thing is, with a little advance thought, any guy can fill that role.

Problem Turnoffs for "Perfect" Guys

You may assume perfect-looking guys have all the high cards. But not so fast. They actually face a few disadvantages with girls.

> ### Crazy Truth 3
> Some qualities of Abercrombie Boy actually turn girls off.

Sure, girls can be visually attracted to a buff guy. But, believe it or not, they also appear to have an automatic suspicion of him. In fact, we learned that most girls don't trust Mr. Perfect-on-the-Outside. They figure he is arrogant and full of himself. They think he'll treat them badly and then move on.

If you're like both of us, you are *so* sad to hear this. *Aw, poor little rich, good-looking, popular dudes...* But we couldn't ignore what so many girls said:

- "All good-looking guys are suspect."
- "If he has a huge ego, we know he'll always need the next hot girl hanging on him."

‣ "I don't want to feel like I have to blow-dry my hair and put on makeup to match his perfection."

‣ "This good-looking guy was a jerk to all my friends. They weren't jealous at all, even though he's attractive, because he was so rude and cocky!"

Of course, not all superattractive guys are jerks. The girls pointed out that when they flock around a good-looking guy they know well, it's because he's simply a good guy, deserving attention for reasons other than his looks.

> Most girls don't trust Mr. Perfect-on-the-Outside. They figure he is arrogant and full of himself.

Smart Moves Girls Wish Every Guy Would Make

We decided to ask what Average Joe can do to set himself apart in the heart of a girl. The girls we interviewed told us. And we're passing on their requests because they asked us to. Guys, they said, would have so much more fun and success with girls if we just *listened* to what girls say on a few important matters.

Are you ready to listen…and act? Taking an honest look at ourselves—and deciding to do something about what we see—is tough work. But it's not rocket science. Call it wising up about girls. Call it growing up. Call it learning how to win. Call it…whatever works for you.

At one point in our survey, we asked girls this question:

SURVEY How should a guy who is trying to make a good impression on a girl spend his free time? (Choose one answer.)

a. In the gym to improve how he looks.

b. In a way that would improve his inner qualities and personality.

If you've been reading carefully, you could predict what most girls chose. "Improve his inner qualities and personality" won with an overwhelming 91 percent of the vote!

So let's get to work. What follow are five smart moves Average Joes can take because they now know what's really going on inside a girl's heart and mind. Read carefully. But read relaxed. Don't feel that you have to become someone you're not. If we talk about humor, for example, don't feel that you have to turn into the class clown if that's not the way you're wired. You could just as easily look for one-on-one opportunities to make a girl smile. It's just that you deserve to be the best *you* you can be around girls.

We think you'll finish this chapter with a much better idea of what you might do to relate better to girls in a way you are comfortable with. Best of all, you'll know that you *can* do it. Because it's such simple stuff.

Smart Move 1: Take humor seriously.

Since three out of four girls said a sense of humor is one of the three most attractive traits in a guy, it's time to take humor seriously. If you are naturally a funny guy, realize just how much the rest of us hate you. If you aren't, don't suddenly try to memorize joke books ("Hey, Megan! So a lawyer, a priest, and a duck walk into a bar…"). The key is to have your radar up for opportunities to make a girl laugh. And remember that humor can be cute or clever without being belly-laugh funny.

If you aren't sure what works for you and what doesn't, take two weeks and watch for what makes girls laugh or smile in different situations. Then take a shot at it yourself. When something amusing happens, tuck it away for later retelling. And while cut-down humor against someone else is almost never appealing, don't be afraid to poke fun at yourself now and then. Girls will notice your sense of humor:

▸ "There's a guy in the band that I like a lot. He wears glasses and has those man boobs—but he's also goofy and humorous and has a great personality. I was looking at him yesterday and thinking, *I could date him.*"

▸ "I'm not very funny, so I'm drawn to a guy who can make me laugh instead of me having to come up with a bunch of nonsense."

Smart Move 2: Bring the fun; be the adventure.

Okay, what's fun (like what's funny) is different for different people. But most of us recognize that fun feeling when it happens. Girls sure do. Goofing around someplace new, playing in the sun, watching a movie you want to talk about afterward, forgetting about anything stressful, the two of you smiling blissful smiles—you know fun when you're having it!

Girls say they love guys with a "let's try something new" attitude. One girl told us: "It's nice to wake up in the morning and not know exactly what's going to happen. Every day is different when you have a guy with a sense of adventure."

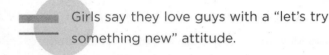

Girls say they love guys with a "let's try something new" attitude.

Smart Move 3: Cut loose with your Inner Gentleman.

Every guy has an Inner Gentleman. No, really. It's just that for some of us it takes a while to get him to show up. *Why?* girls wonder. Well, most of us start out being self-centered and immature. And some of us don't grow up around adults who are thoughtful or respectful of others, especially of women. But somewhere along the way, sharp guys realize that gentlemanly conduct is powerful stuff in opposite-sex relationships.

Guys who don't learn that lesson pay a price. (We're talking about guys who don't offer to carry things, open doors, or speak politely to adults, especially parents of their favorite girl.) They get ignored, dumped, or end up in one unhappy relationship after another.

But average guys can suddenly get very attractive if they're willing to treat a girl so she feels noticed and cared for:

▸ "When a guy is gentlemanly, it shows he has respect for you. When he's not, it really makes you appreciate the ones who are."

▸ "This guy in my neighborhood is so considerate. He's always trying to find ways to make my life easier or happier, and he's very giving. That kind of thoughtfulness will carry a guy far."

One girl told us about a clueless clod named David. "Over the summer, this guy David was at the pool, and I was sitting next to him on the picnic table," she wrote. "We were both starving, and there was this family that had a couple pieces of pizza left at their table. He went over and asked if he could have some."

At this point the girl is thinking, *My brave hunter-provider!* But here's what happened next: "David came back with two slices, which I quickly found out were both for him. He knew I was starving too, but he ate them both right in front of me!" (Uh, nicely done, David.)

"My opinion of David went into the toilet," the girl said. "If a guy wants to be attractive, he can't just think selfishly. He needs to learn to become a gentleman with girls."

Smart Move 4: Step up to confidence.

This is a tough one only if you struggle with self-confidence (that would be 98 percent of all sane teenagers). But part of being a man is learning to show courage and strength even if you don't always feel it. Girls just prefer being around a confident guy. He's calm and polite. He looks them in the eye. He's okay with who he is. He's in charge (or at least he seems to be).

The payoff for the girl is huge. First off, she can relax and feel safe. And she can get interested. Hey, we all sense that confidence comes from courage and strength. What girl isn't going to be attracted to that?

Grandmas all over the world are right about this one. They're always shaking a bony finger in some young man's face and saying things like, "Stand up straight!" and, "Walk into that room like you own the place, sonny!" and, "Look people in the eye when you talk to them."

Quite a few girls reported that when a guy won't talk with them or look them in the eyes, they feel insecure. One cute high-school girl told us, "If a guy doesn't ever look in my eyes when he's around me, I feel like there must be something wrong with me!"

I (Jeff) will admit that as a teen I wasn't the most confident guy in the world when it came to girls. I was pretty outgoing and had a lot of friends who were girls, but as you have already seen with my Diane story, I was sure I would look like a total idiot trying to take a friendship to the next level. You may not have that same paralyzing feeling, but if you do, we've got some ideas for you that might help.

One cute high-school girl told us, "If a guy doesn't ever look in my eyes when he's around me, I feel like there must be something wrong with me!"

Here are some ideas for avoiding "girl paralysis":

▸ *Remember who you are.* And you are who *God* says you are, not who you might suspect you are when you're feeling like a total idiot. God created you for a reason—a good one. Be who you really are, not who you think you should be to impress a girl.

▸ *Don't listen to the lies.* A big part of self-confidence is how you carry yourself—and that starts with how you think about yourself. If you think you're only worth getting rejected, when you try to ask a girl out, you're likely to shake like a blob of warm Jell-O in the sink just before the disposal sucks it away. (And believe it or not, one of your best resources for combating age-old lies can be your age-old parents. Just don't tell them we called them old! Ask them how they overcame insecurities and wrong thinking and learned to step out in confidence. That must've happened at some point because you're here, right?)

▸ *Take a deep breath and take a risk.* We like to remember the Bible verse that says, "In quietness and confidence is your strength." In every focus group, we heard girls say things like, "Guys don't realize that when they take a risk to ask us out, we'll respect them more, not less!" Yes, it is a risk, but what's the worst that could happen? If a girl turns you down, we promise it won't rip a hole in the space-time continuum that will suck you into an alternate universe from which you'll never escape. (Although it may feel like that at the time.) Take the risk. No matter what, you have a bright future ahead.

▸ *Clean up your act.* It's hard to feel or be cool when you're a slob. Standing out from the crowd can be appealing to girls. But standing out because you have bad personal hygiene is *not* the way to a girl's heart.

▸ *Take the initiative instead of being passive.* Don't force her to make all the decisions. One common complaint we heard from the girls was, "When we're out, I don't want a guy who says, 'I don't care… Whatever you want to do.'"

▸ *"Do it afraid" and the confidence will follow.* As a film director, I (Eric) love stories of daring and courage. But in most of those stories, the heroes are ordinary guys who *feel* terrified but still choose to *act* bravely. They do it afraid: they gut it out, doing what needs to be done when others won't. Confidence follows. And so does the princess's attention! As one girl wrote about confidence, "Fake it till you make it!"

▸ *Be real.* Once you've known a girl for a while—whether as a friend or a girlfriend—trust her enough to share your real feelings, even in areas where you are less than confident. That honesty is where superficiality stops and a real friendship begins.

Take a risk. If a girl turns you down, we promise it won't rip a hole in the space-time continuum that will suck you into an alternate universe from which you'll never escape.

Smart Move 5: Live your faith.

Remember that many girls ranked a genuine faith as being the number one most appealing characteristic in a guy. And, interestingly, those who didn't rank it that high never viewed it as a negative.

We would never recommend that you use the "I'm so religious" angle to snag a girl. But if you're a Christ follower like us, there's a lot to be learned here. For one thing, we can be encouraged that we don't have to hide from girls what matters most to us spiritually. Besides, what's to be gained by hiding your faith so you can get a girl who doesn't value it in the first place? That's a shortsighted, hypocritical, cheesy strategy that will only land you in a place and with a person you'll regret.

But there's something else to learn too: girls are pretty smart, and if you say one thing and do another, look out! You'll come off as the fake you are. The keyword here is *genuine*.

Genuine faith starts on the inside and works itself out from there. If you're a Christian, *genuine* means you have given Christ first place in your life. *Genuine* means that what you say you believe and what you do with your life—your talk, your values, uh, where your hands go when you're on a date—all line up. A dating resource we especially like is *Dateable: Are You? Are They?* by Justin Lookadoo and Hayley DiMarco.

"You Can Do It, Waterboy!"

It's time to recap what we've learned:

▸ Crazy Truth 1. Surprisingly, *girls look beyond looks.* They just aren't as visual as guys when it comes to picking out a potential romantic interest.

▸ Crazy Truth 2. Instead, *inner qualities count more* for girls. Who you are and how you treat them, for example, have the biggest appeal.

▸ Crazy Truth 3. *Rich, good-looking jerks may win early, but they usually lose later.* Smart girls are automatically suspicious of the arrogance of Abercrombie Boys. So who you are as a person and how you treat a girl will make all the difference.

And all this adds up to the huge promise for Average Joes—what we call Crazy Truth 4.

Crazy Truth 4
When an average guy puts the truth about girls to work in his life, his great inner qualities will shine through—and girls will notice.

As the weird guy in the stands in the movie said, "You can do it, waterboy!" We hope the warnings and advice of hundreds of girls have helped you regain any hope you've lost along your journey. That's why we came up with our Five Smart Moves for Average Joes.

Master these, Joe, and attractive, high-quality girls will be whispering your name outside your window. Well, maybe not. But now that you "get" these things, you'll suddenly have much more confidence, and your life with girls will get a *lot* more interesting.

3

WHY GOOD GIRLS
LIKE BAD BOYS

*Understanding a girl's greatest secret
fear—and what you can do about it*

Zack is the all-American nice guy, and Ashley—a girl who hangs with his crowd—thinks so too. Zack plays sports, has friends, and is clean, polite, and fun. He loves his parents, goes to church on Sundays, and spent most of last weekend helping Ashley with her math homework.

Actually, Zack is secretly nuts about Ashley. He and Ashley have so much in common. And he figured things were going his way last weekend when she let him know how much she appreciates his help and enjoys hanging with him.

But then Sunday night, as they were putting their books away, Ashley told Zack who *she* is secretly nuts about.

And it's not him.

Zack went home hurt and confused. Hurt because Ashley's heart was with someone else. Confused because that someone else was Evan Knight.

Evan Knight?! Evan is not a nice guy. He's an arrogant, foul-mouthed, hard-partying guy who hates his parents and has had run-ins with the police. Evan hauls a beat-up guitar everywhere he goes, scribbling angry lyrics in class like he's the next Kurt Cobain.

"Give me a break," groans Zack.

Oh, and let's not forget that Evan flirts with Ashley every chance he gets. Middle of the hallway with five people listening is fine. Middle of the cafeteria with twenty people watching is even better.

What's Zack supposed to think about Ashley's new crush? Why would a smart, sensitive girl like Ashley look right past him and fall for such an obvious loser?

Plenty of guys we talk to have been in Zack's situation. They've watched good girls get sucked into relationships with bad boys, and they've wondered what gives. Have you? We're talking girls who know better, study hard, and want to have a loving family of their own someday. They say they want a nice guy, but their actions suggest otherwise. We're standing right next to them, and what do they do? Give their heart to some train wreck waiting to happen.

Even filmmakers have tuned in to this strange phenomenon. For example, in *The Princess Diaries* (admit it, you watched it), Mia begins as a dowdy wallflower who is so invisible that she literally gets sat on. One of the only breaks in her dull life is dreaming about kissing the school's best-known bad boy. Josh, a good-looking guy, is so into himself that any guy watching the movie just wants to put the hurt on him. Mia hardly notices her best friend's brother, a not-as-flashy nice guy named Michael. After Mia finds out she's a princess, Josh all of a sudden starts hitting on her. And she falls for it. She even breaks a date with Michael—who's been kind, helpful, and attentive to her all year—because she gets a better offer from Josh.

In this chapter we will try to find answers to this infuriating female behavior. (Should we call it Black Knight Syndrome?) Right off, we'll tell you that the behavior, while weird and annoying, is not that big of a deal *compared with the huge insight it will lead us to.* Think of it as Zack's problem leading to your opportunity. Or think of Ashley's behavior as a symptom of something much deeper and a lot more important that every young man needs to know about. Including you. We guarantee that by the end of this chapter, you'll experience a big "aha!" about two very important questions you aren't even asking right now:

1. What is it about bad boys that attracts good (otherwise smart) girls?
2. What secret need in her drives such insanity?

Once you see what's really going on, you'll understand how to relate to girls better. And here's something even more important, a truth that all the Evan Knights of the world miss completely: God made guys to answer a girl's secret need in ways that encourage, honor, and protect her.

Once you discover what her secret need is, you'll get what we mean.

Dreaming About Black Knights

To figure out what happened to Zack, we asked girls to tell us exactly what it is about the Evan Knights of the world that makes them such unlikely and—let's just say it—*unworthy* girl magnets.

SURVEY	Many guys are puzzled why girls sometimes seem to go for the "bad boy." What personality attributes might be attractive to you in a "bad boy"...? Choose all that apply.

"Being self-confident, adventuresome, and having other positive attributes"	96%
• Self-confident / self-assured	81%
• Adventuresome / spontaneous	72%
• Protective	63%
• Leader that other guys look up to	55%
• Decisive	43%
"Being edgy"	**75%**
• Risk taker / breaks out of the mold / pushes the limits	46%
• Not afraid of anybody	41%
• Edgy	38%
• Smart mouth	10%
• Likes to be the center of attention	9%
"Being rebellious, cocky, or having other dark attributes"	**21%**
• Rebellious / rule breaker / defies authority	16%
• Cocky	9%
• Foul language	5%

0% 50% 100%

Note: The top line of each section shows the percentage of girls who chose one or more of the answers in that section. Percentages do not total 100 percent because girls could choose more than one answer.

We found two big surprises in these results and the quotes that follow. First, girls are overwhelmingly attracted to bad boys because of their positive qualities. Okay, *perceived* positive qualities. Almost all of the girls (96 percent) see certain positive qualities—confidence, adventure, and protection, for example—in bad guys that really capture their attention. Second, we noticed how few of the girls were actually attracted to behavior that we usually think of as normal for bad guys. Normal as in "cocky," "rebellious / defies authority," or "foul language." Only one in five picked these as attractive.

Look at what the girls told us, and you'll get the picture:

- "A bad boy isn't afraid to stick up for you. It shows a real love, that he cares."
- "I'm predictable, and I want the bad boy to bring out the spontaneity and adventure in me."
- "I like the guys who aren't afraid to talk to girls, to ask them out, to joke around, to do something on the edge a little."
- "Bad boys aren't clingy."
- "The bad boy doesn't care what other people think of him. That's why he is the way he is. Whereas every teenage girl cares so deeply about what other people think of her, so being with him is a kind of freedom."
- "I like a guy who's a little wild because you can live on the wild side without actually doing it—without the consequences. You live vicariously through him when he's going to jump his bike over five buses, but you don't have to walk around on crutches when he breaks his leg."

Either you're really confused now, or you already read chapter 2 about the appeal of Average Joe. What sticks out all over the place here is that a girl's wish list when it comes to boys doesn't change much. The qualities she's looking for in any guy—whether it's Abercrombie Boy, Average Joe, or Bad-Dude Evan Knight—are about the same. It's right there in front of us, in familiar words like these:

- *confidence*
- *fun*
- *adventure*
- *decisive*
- *doesn't let shyness freeze him*

The previous chapter mentioned one attractive trait that isn't part of a bad boy's playbook: thoughtfulness. In a minute we'll address why girls seem willing to trade this away. But for now just realize that not even one girl said she was attracted to the dark side for reasons like, " 'Cause the drugs are free, man!" or, "You go to better parties," or, "Well, I hate my dog, my dad, my school, and you too, so it just makes sense to hang with the dark side."

"I like the guys who aren't afraid to talk to girls, to ask them out, to joke around, to do something on the edge a little."

The girls were all looking for something else—something any guy can deliver by the truckload if he pays attention and is willing to try something new.

Learning from the Dark Side

Take a look at a story we heard from a college girl we'll call Jacki. As you read it, don't just react to the guy's see-through moves. Notice instead the effect his moves have on Jacki and her comments about why she was so tempted.

I was driving down the freeway when this "bad boy" in a sports car pulled up next to me. He gave me a big smile out the window. Then I noticed he was writing something on a piece of paper. When he held it up, it said, "You are gorgeous."

Hey, every girl likes hearing that! So I smiled. A minute later, when I looked back over, he was holding up another sign. It said, "Next exit. One drink."

I shook my head no. But the guy didn't give up. His next sign read, "If you hate me, I'll leave. I promise."

Then he held up the second sign again. "Next exit. One drink."

I admit, at that moment I was unbelievably tempted to accept. He had such a bold, exciting bad-boy thing going on, and I have to tell you it played with my head. My life is so conservative and even boring sometimes. Here was this exciting guy in a nice car tempting me to have a little adventure. I didn't do it, but I can see why girls take risks with strangers or want the bad boy. Even though your head is warning you about possible danger, you just feel like you're being swept off your feet.

The crazy thing is that we know exactly what these sports-car-driving, off-the-feet-sweeping bad boys are thinking. And it's not, *Gee, if this fine young lady will get in my car, I'll put on my Mozart collection and listen for hours as she talks about what's really on her mind.* "On her mind"—are you kidding? We know the guy just wants to see what's under her clothes.

But, believe it or not, most girls don't know this. Or if they do, they still like the feeling of what's happening so much that they may actually consider going with it. Most girls told us that in Jacki's situation they'd be tempted to think, *Wow, he notices me, and he's really attracted to me as a person. And if it's just my looks, oh well, at least he thinks I'm gorgeous. And we'll have fun!*

What can Average Joes and Overlooked Zacks learn from this powerful fact? Clearly, what's going on inside Jacki is *not* what's going on inside Mr. Bad Dude in Sports Car. And, clearly, some very real, very deep need is eating away at Jacki and making her vulnerable to getting swept away...by the wrong guy.

And what is that very real, very deep need in a girl? Well, we thought we'd ask a boatload of girls. And that brings us to part two of the picture and the most important part of this chapter.

> "Even though your head is warning you about possible danger, you just feel like you're being swept off your feet."

The Question That's Secretly Killing Her

When we pressed the girls further on what was so appealing about bad guys who pursue them, they agreed that it mostly has to do with what's going on inside them as girls and only a little to do with the guys.

What's going on in them, we discovered, is the gnawing, subconscious fear that they are not attractive or appealing—that, ultimately, they are not lovable. More surprising yet is that this terrible insecurity attacks even the girls everyone else thinks of as beautiful and popular.

We'll show you in a minute how a smart girl gets from the secret question, "Will anyone really love me?" to a dumb choice like, "Evan is so hot!" But before we do that, let's look more closely at what the girls said about their hidden insecurity.

SURVEY In which of the following areas, if any, do you feel less than confident or question how others view you? (Choose all that apply.)

"Whether I'm liked"	**75%**
• Whether I'm being talked about behind my back	
• Whether the guys I want to like me do like me	
• Whether I'm really liked and accepted for who I am by friends and acquaintances	
• Social status / popularity / how well I fit in	
"How I look"	**72%**
• Body image	
• Whether I'm pretty	
• Clothes / how I dress	
"Who I am"	**58%**
• Whether I'm really liked and accepted for who I am by friends and acquaintances	
• Whether I'm valuable and unique as a person	
• My skills and abilities	
• Intelligence / how I'm doing in school	
"None of the above; I am confident in all these areas."	**9%**

Note: The top line of each section shows the percentage of girls who chose one or more of the answers in that section. Percentages do not total 100 percent because girls could choose more than one answer.

During our interviews and test surveys at malls, we noticed that even really attractive girls confessed that they weren't happy with how they looked. For girls this part of life must feel harsh. How many guys realize that most girls they pass in the hall are torn up inside by deep doubts about a basic question: *Am I attractive, special, and lovable?* * Yet the survey shows that's exactly what's happening. *Nine out of ten girls* feel insecure in at least one important area. And three out of four girls are especially insecure about the two biggies:

▸ whether they are liked for *who they are*

▸ whether *how they look* is appealing

For sure, we guys have our own secret fears. But these tend to be more performance oriented. We're afraid we'll do or say something stupid or suffer a humiliating defeat in front of thousands of cheering spectators—or one pretty girl.

With girls, the deep insecurity is different. They ask themselves, *Will anyone like me? Does he think I'm attractive? What do people really think of me?* And what's more, in a fundamental way they tend to particularly look to guys for reassurance about the answers to these questions. Look at what the girls told us:

▸ "Whether or not you are attractive can only be affirmed by guys."

▸ "We measure our worth by who's attracted to us."

▸ "If we're honest, every girl will tell you she's not always secure that she's an okay person."

▸ "One of my greatest fears is that I won't be enough to satisfy him, so that he has to go elsewhere."

---

* Now, don't try to solve this problem by running up to that cute girl and saying, "I think you're attractive, special, and lovable." You may get slapped.

▸ "If a guy doesn't like me, I must not be likable. There's something in me that's rejectable."

In case you're thinking these comments were coming from homely, pudding-brained girls who never leave the house, we refer you again to www.foryoungmenonly.com to see the girls we interviewed. Not only can you count on our survey being statistically valid, you can also know that a huge majority of the girls we talked to in our focus groups were absolutely impressive in so many ways.

The insecurity the girls describe here helps explain why a lot of pretty girls put up with a lot of ugly treatment at the hands of boyfriends. Jeff's wife, Shaunti, can still remember such a situation with a roommate at college. This girl was attractive and fun loving—and spent years dating a guy who treated her poorly.

When one of this girl's friends confronted her about why she put up with the guy, she answered, "Well, it's better than being alone."

To which the friend exclaimed, "Why would you assume you'd be alone?!"

By now you're asking, "But what does a girl's insecurity have to do with her weakness for bad boys?" Or maybe you've already put it together, because the clues are right there in plain sight.

This terrible insecurity attacks even the girls everyone else thinks of as beautiful and popular.

Bad Boy Finally Gets an A

Ashley probably fell for Bad-Dude Evan instead of the helpful and recently showered Zack because Evan gave the best answer to her big question. Remember it? It's the question *every* girl is asking: *Am I attractive, special, and lovable?*

When it comes to answering this question, bad boys often do a better job of doing and saying what makes a girl feel noticed. When Ashley's around nonassertive nice-guy Zack, she mostly gets either mixed signals or silence. But around a cocky bad boy like Evan, Ashley is bound to get surprised by some outrageous flirtation or delighted by some bold move that tells her he does notice her.

Of course, the rest of us want to throw up when we see Bad Dude hitting on a girl. And sure, sometimes he does go over the top. But still, he gets a lot of things right:

- He's taking the lead.
- He's making a decision.
- He's taking a risk.
- He's showing confidence.

Remember all those important inner qualities? When Evan makes his move, he lets Ashley know (or believe at least for a minute) that she has him under her spell. He makes her thumper wildly thump. Suddenly she feels *very* likable.

Feeling likable is a thrill that melts a girl's insecurity like ice cubes in the Sahara.

BACKSTAGE...

 Bad boys sometimes give the best answer to her question: *Am I attractive, special, and lovable?*

Again: The Secret of Confidence

There's more to all this than just attention and flirtation, of course. When a guy is confident, a girl feels the strength she's looking for. She thinks, *This guy isn't afraid of anybody,* or, *This guy knows how to take charge.* And she is deeply reassured when such a fearless leader is interested in *her.* (Yes, we can read your mind: you want to be that guy!) Here are some typical comments from girls:

▸ "We want the confident guy because we want to feel protected, like we can go to him for anything."

▸ "When you're uncertain with yourself, we become uncertain with you. Deep down, every girl wants a man who can take the lead and take care of her."

▸ "I think we're secretly wanting to draw on a guy's strength. We're attracted to strength when we feel weak. It's like that line from the movie: 'You complete me.'"

▸ "We want the knight but will sometimes go for the black knight. Especially since we secretly don't believe the white knight would ever really go for us."

Fueling all these needs and wants is a girl's secret insecurity. The guy who gets that fact (whatever his other qualities are like) will understand how to make a girl's day and even win her heart.

You might be wondering if we're going to advise you to quit being so nice and start being bad. (If *you're* not wondering, your mother or youth pastor definitely is.) Relax. There's no reason for you to act like some bad boy who's got more attitude and fewer brain cells than your average hamster. Because there's something else we have to tell you…

"When you're uncertain with yourself, we become uncertain with you. Deep down, every girl wants a man who can take the lead and take care of her."

Zack Throws One More Punch (Nicely, of Course)

Confession: a little earlier we told you the truth but not the whole truth. (Jeff's a lawyer—what did you expect?) On the survey question on page 44, we told you we asked, "What personality attributes might be attractive in a 'bad boy'…?" But that wasn't the whole question.

Our reason for this cruel ploy was that we wanted you to notice that what a girl sees—or thinks she sees—in a bad boy is strikingly similar to what she sees in *any* guy she's attracted to. So now here's the *whole* question the way we actually asked it, including the part we left out earlier: "What personality attributes might be attractive in a 'bad boy' that (if he also had them) would make a 'nice guy' even more attractive to you?"

With every one of their answers about bad boys, the girls were really telling the Zacks of the world how to drop the Evan Knights of the world with a sharp left hook (politely delivered, of course). Hands down, girls say that the best possible combination is a guy who has a fun, adventuresome attitude toward life *and* will confidently pursue a girl he likes—but without the pushy, cocky rebelliousness that defines the bad boy. In fact, fewer than one girl in five had any interest in the dark stuff. Here are three sample comments:

▸ "We'd rather have 'nice.' It's just that if that means boring, predictable, no adventure, no confidence—forget it. We'll go for the edgy guy."

▸ "Most of the time, a guy's appeal isn't about the dark side or anything having to do with looks. It's about the vibe you give off. If you're confident (or at least can fake it well), can hold down a conversation, seem interested, throw in some jokes—*WhaBam!* You've just charmed a lady!"

▸ "We really do want the great guy who will hold up over time, not the smoking, drinking party boy who's getting in trouble."

The obvious lesson is that Zack has every chance in the world to get Ashley's attention—if he will apply what he knows about how girls are wired and is willing to improve his serve in a few key areas.

The best possible combination is a guy who has a fun, adventuresome attitude toward life *and* will confidently pursue a girl he likes—but without the pushy, cocky rebelliousness that defines the bad boy.

Wisdom for White Knights

We're ready now to lay down some advice on how decent guys can better respond to a girl's insecurities, and we'll summarize what we've learned from the bad guys.

Understand her insecurities; protect her heart.

All guys fear not measuring up in some way. Draw on those feelings to understand how a girl might feel in the areas where she's most vulnerable. Remember, she's going to be especially sensitive about how she looks and how likable she is. So look for ways to genuinely affirm and compliment her. (Oh, and just so you know, the girls said "you're so hot" backfires. Instead, tell her she's fun to be with. Or if she's bummed that she forgot her makeup, casually remark, "You don't need any!") Girls told us that humor also helps, but only if you're laughing *with* her, not *at* her.

Because of what you now know about a girl's deepest hopes and fears, you have a responsibility to watch out for her heart. One girl told us this:

> It's cool when a guy will protect you, because we often don't feel that way at home or with our girlfriends. We can be a pretty strong, capable personality and still feel a bit unsettled about moving forward in the big bad world. So when you get the sense that a guy is really looking out for you—physically and emotionally—it satisfies that secret fear.

Protection is the opposite of playing with her emotions to get what you want. You can still be confident, fun, and thoughtful without leading girls on. You wouldn't want a girl to be careless with *your* heart, would you? So do your best not to be careless with hers.

Take some risks.

We've pointed out how a girl's wish list for guy qualities doesn't really change—just the package he comes in. So take a minute to review what girls told us about those qualities and the tips we passed along (see pages 31–38).

Like us, girls get a rush from doing fun things, sharing an adventure, and feeling the thrill of freedom. Where a bad boy will offer an emotionally dangerous path, the girls we talked to said they'd much prefer being swept off on a fun adventure by a nicer guy. But that means you, the nice guy, have to take action. Maybe offer to teach her to snowboard one day on the youth group ski trip. Or get a group together for laser tag. Convince her to go on the scariest roller coaster. With you.

And listen: we're *not* talking about making stupid, dangerous choices. (You've probably heard the joke, "What's the last thing a redneck says right before he dies?" "Hey, y'all, watch *this*!") If you can't come up with an idea, ask girls you know—or the girl you're interested in—to tell you what they think is fun and exciting.

Where a bad boy will offer an emotionally dangerous path, the girls we talked to said they'd much prefer being swept off on a fun adventure by a nicer guy.

Pursue her.

And we don't mean chasing her around on the playground the way you did when you were seven. Girls who were secretly drawn to the bad boy all said they responded to his focused attention. He takes the first step and lets her know he's interested in her. She feels wanted,

noticed, pursued. Pursuing a girl is as easy as saying, "A bunch of us are going to the movies. I'd love for you to join us."

Have the courage to stand up and put your heart on the line. Focus on her in a positive, affirming way. Sincerely desire to know her better, not just get something from her. You'll definitely make an impression.

If you're already a twosome, pursuing despite the risk can be as simple as not letting her withdraw during an argument but instead trying to find out what is wrong (she might say, "It's none of your business"). You're risking rejection—and to her that's a good thing. To her, that's you giving chase.

If you're not dating, risking rejection by asking for some time together is a big step. At some point in our lives, most of us guys have stared at a phone for hours, afraid to call a cute girl. But ask *in person* if you really want to score points. Give it a shot. When you get so nervous that your words come out backward and you walk into the wall, she's likely to think you're the most adorable guy she's ever seen.

Have the courage to stand up and put your heart on the line.

Dark Knights Thought Problem

So what have we learned about girls, dark dudes, and insecurity? Think of it as a thought problem, then take it one logical step at a time so no one gets lost.

▸ Thought 1: Even a seemingly confident girl secretly fears that she isn't special, attractive, or lovable.

▸ Thought 2: When a guy boldly pays attention to her, she feels wanted. She thinks, *Wow, I must be special after all!* She gets that "Wow!" feeling whether the guy is a good guy, a sleazy guy, or SpongeBob SquarePants. Well, almost.

▸ Thought 3: Problem is, during the teen years, it's often the Dark Knight with a lot of attitude and not so many brain cells who throws off strong confidence vibes.

These three thoughts add up to a golden opportunity for ordinary guys who can't figure out why they can't get a girl's attention. See, you don't need to pierce yourself with chain link or fire off obscenities like a drill sergeant. You don't need to pretend you're Kurt Cobain reincarnated. You don't even need to hate your mother. You just need to be you.

You just need to be you.

Now that you understand the secret question that is burning in every girl's soul, you can encourage girls by stepping up to the plate and being the man you were designed to be—and the man they are really looking for.

4

WHEN GIRLS STOP MAKING SENSE

*A code breaker's guide
to baffling female behavior*

iPod nano & You
A story in four days

Day One: You plunk down some cash for a new iPod nano. Of course, you don't look at the manual. Duh! You just turn it on, move your thumb around on the click wheel, navigate through the menu, download some music, and within minutes, you're listening to your favorite tunes.

Day Two: You head out for a run, thumb on click wheel, listening to your favorite workout tunes…

Day Three: You hit the books, thumb on click wheel, listening to your favorite study tunes…

Day Four: You walk through town, thumb on click wheel…

Well, you get the picture. That iPod is always an iPod—no surprises, no dead air. One click and you're listening to your favorite tunes.

Thank you, Steve Jobs.

Girl & You
Another story in four days

Day One: You and she have a fabulous time hanging out at her house, then do a movie and smoothies. She smiles, listens to your stories, laughs at your jokes. You hold hands. Those poor suckers with nothing to hold but an iPod. Life is good.

Day Two: You and she have a fabulous time hanging out after school. She smiles, laughs, listens to your stories (probably the same ones), laughs at your jokes (even though they're lame). You hold hands. Life is good.

Day Three: You have a weird time hanging out with her and a bunch of friends at Starbucks. And she's not smiling. At least not at *you*. She's not listening or laughing either. You can't find her hand. Life is…weird.

Day Four: What in the world happened on Day Three? Is something wrong with your new girlfriend? Or is something wrong with you?

You don't have a clue! You shuffle home alone. Those lucky suckers who just have an iPod to figure out. Life stinks.

Oh, if girls could just be like iPods! Everything would be so much simpler. But they're not (okay, that's a good thing). Girls are complicated…and *so* confusing. One day they say one thing; the next day the exact opposite. Sometimes they seem perfectly normal, logical, understandable. Then…*whap!* Your sweet thing goes into a sulk. Or turns into a flamethrower. And you're wondering what happened.

Well, what *did* happen? *Is she crazy?* you wonder. *Did I do something stupid? Should I try to work things out—or should I run?*

That's what this chapter is about.

 Girls are complicated…and *so* confusing.

Cracking the Female Response Code

Throwing caution to the wind, we set out to ask girls if they thought they always made sense. No, really. We figured we might as well get right to the point—and get them to admit the truth. The truth as in, "No. Half the time we're crazed mutants."

But here's what happened instead. As we listened to the girls in the focus groups and shopping malls, we were stunned to find them saying that *almost every seemingly random behavior by a girl is actually logical. It happens for a reason.*

We didn't believe a word of it. But just so you can look at the evidence yourself, read our question and their responses:

Many guys believe that there aren't really rational reasons when a girl's attitudes, actions, or words change from day to day. Which of the following is true of you? (Choose one.)

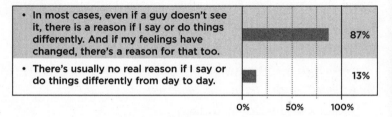

• In most cases, even if a guy doesn't see it, there is a reason if I say or do things differently. And if my feelings have changed, there's a reason for that too.	87%
• There's usually no real reason if I say or do things differently from day to day.	13%

Add it up. Nearly nine out of ten girls say they behave like they do for a reason. With numbers like that, we decided to look more closely. And what we found was both a big shock and a big relief. The more we listened, the more we realized that (a) the girls weren't messing with us and that (b) they just might know something we didn't.

Right about then our natural genius kicked in, and we had an amazing insight: if reasons actually do exist, then a code for understanding them would exist. Call it the Female Response Code. Furthermore, we brilliantly concluded, if a guy took the time to crack this code, he would know how to make his personal "Girl & You" story have a much better ending than the one you just read.

Are you brave enough to try it? If you are, we think you'll learn some things you never would have imagined.

We should first point out that code breaking in wartime can be hazardous duty. (For some reason, most guys agree that war analogies fit nicely in this chapter.) Just as the code breakers in World War II had to get dangerously close to enemy lines in order to hear their radio transmissions, so you must take risks to listen carefully to what a girl is saying. And—this is critical—you must listen to and observe her confusing words and actions, believing that there is a reason (and thus a code) that ordinary guys like you—and us—can figure out.

We think the risk is worth it. Once you know how to break the code, we guarantee that your life with girls (and later with your wife) will improve dramatically.

> As we listened to the girls in the focus groups and shopping malls, we were stunned to find them saying that almost every seemingly random behavior by a girl is actually logical.

What's Wrong with Her Today?

Your first step is logical but hypothetical. You have to consider the possibility that a girl's feelings are coming from somewhere—in other words, that there is a reason behind the feelings. And if you can figure out where that somewhere is, then you'll be on your way to breaking the seemingly random code.

"Oh, great!" you're saying. "You're calling a feeling a *reason*? No way! A reason has to be logical—and most of the time a girl's feelings are like chunks of banana being flung from a blender."

Well, yes and no. As you're about to find out.

Hundreds of girls helped us see that there are four answers to the question, "What's wrong with *her* today?"

1. something you've done, even if you don't realize you did it
2. something about her circumstances (it's not about you)
3. something that's going on inside her
4. hormone poisoning

Our survey results show that a girl's irrational behavior is nearly always rooted in an important reality, whether physical, emotional, or circumstantial. As one girl put it, "We can't always tell the guy what's happening, but there usually is a logical explanation for what may look like strange or moody behavior."

But code breaking takes time. You need patience. And a steely determination to u-n-d-e-r-s-t-a-n-d. Take a look.

Category 1: She's reacting to something you've done, even if you don't realize you did it.

Let's be honest. We guys can do and say things that get a strong reaction in a girl. Often, though, we don't even know we did or said those things. And since we're clueless, we blame her for a reaction that we caused.

The girls we talked to tried to be helpful. We'll give you two examples:

She feels hurt because of something you said or did.

As you now know from the previous chapter—and from experience!—girls have sensitivities that guys can easily trigger. When my (Eric's) wife, Lisa, and I were in college, the rules were much stricter, and guys and girls couldn't be in each other's dorms very often. One day I visited her dorm hall, spent a little time talking in her room, then went down the hall to say hi to some of the other girls. I ended up spending quite some time in one room that housed four girls, and by the time I got back to Lisa's, she was gone. I was a little sad about that because she and I had gone out a few times, and I was hoping to hang out with her. Her roommate told me to try the library.

I went to the library, and sure enough, there was Lisa. I thought she'd be happy to see me, but she was actually kind of cold to me. That night at dinner she was equally aloof. *What in the world is going on?* I wondered. Where was the fun, bubbly girl I had taken on a date the previous Friday?

Well, I found out later—much later—that she had been expecting me to spend most of my limited time with her, and she was hurt and jealous that I had spent so much time with the other girls. But she eventually confessed that she couldn't tell me that because it would have seemed too forward and clingy.

Aha! So the seemingly random moodiness did have a rational basis after all. Unfortunately, the basis was me. Duh!

She feels <u>angry because of something you said or did.</u>

During the writing of this book, my (Eric's) daughter Hannah, happened to be looking at a guy friend's Facebook page, and she saw that he had bragged to someone about "scoring with a girl" in our neighborhood. Hannah was horrified because she knew that she was this guy's only girl friend in our neighborhood, and nothing remotely close to "scoring" had happened.

Hannah was so angry at the guy that she was unable to face him for three days. And he couldn't figure out why she had become so distant. When they finally talked, he admitted to posting a lie. "Guys do that," he said. "We just brag and lie sometimes. I'm really sorry." He was ashamed to be the cause of Hannah's three days of misery, and now he also understood why she had suddenly avoided him. There was a reason for the random.

We're happy that the guy got enlightened. But he should count himself lucky that his enlightenment didn't come at the cost of a beatdown from Hannah's other guy friends.

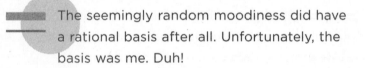

The seemingly random moodiness did have a rational basis after all. Unfortunately, the basis was me. Duh!

Category 2: She is reacting to something about her circumstances (it's not about you).

Look at the fascinating answers we got on the survey:

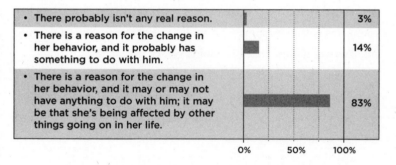

SURVEY Suppose a guy sees a girl acting one way toward him on Monday but a completely different way on Tuesday. In your opinion, which of the following is the most likely explanation? (Choose one.)

• There probably isn't any real reason.	3%
• There is a reason for the change in her behavior, and it probably has something to do with him.	14%
• There is a reason for the change in her behavior, and it may or may not have anything to do with him; it may be that she's being affected by other things going on in her life.	83%

0%   50%   100%

More than eight in ten girls emphasized that a change in behavior toward a guy may simply be because she is being affected by something completely different, something he doesn't know about or didn't notice. One girl in a focus group—we'll call her Jessie—gave us a good example.

On Saturday night, Jessie and her boyfriend, Rob, were sitting on the couch at Jessie's parents' house watching a movie. Rob put his arm around Jessie and drew her closer. She smiled and snuggled in tighter, enjoying the attention. But the next day, when Rob was back again, watching a football game with Jessie on that same couch, he tried the same snuggly move and got a cold shoulder. *What's up with that?* he wondered, and he felt frustration and anger as he thought about her inconsistent behavior.

Little did he know, Jessie had spotted her mother gardening right outside the open window. She had backed away from Rob because she was uncomfortable displaying affection in front of her parents. Her parents knew she and Rob were committed to avoiding sexual situations, but she didn't want them to wonder. And since her mom was within earshot, she couldn't talk about it. She could only pull away and hope that Rob didn't get too offended.

"I was so irritated with him," Jessie recalls, "because he wasn't picking up on my clues that this just wasn't the time for cuddling."

See what we mean? There was a reason for the randomness, but the guy wasn't looking for it.

> "I was so irritated with him," Jessie recalls, "because he wasn't picking up on my clues."

Category 3: She's reacting to something that's going on inside her—and may be testing you as a result.

It makes sense that what's troubling a girl inside might impact how she reacts on the outside. Including how she reacts to a guy, even if he has nothing to do with what's going on.

Unfortunately, as we showed you in chapter 3, one common thing that goes on in a teenage girl's life is insecurity. A girl who feels insecure about, for example, whether you care for her as much as you say you do is likely to put you to a little test. (Oh boy, a pop quiz!)

One girl in a focus group told us about how she tested a guy she secretly liked. One day she casually asked him, "Have you ever considered asking Kara out?" She was thrilled when he answered, "Actually, I was going to ask *you* out." We'd say he passed her test. Especially since all the girls in that focus group practically fainted with delight when they heard that story.

Another girl described a pull-him-in-push-him-away game to test a boy's commitment. "I throw out a little verbal dart to see how easily I can send him running," she said. "It sounds terrible, but if it's real easy for him to run, he obviously doesn't care much about me. So I don't want him."

Confused? Feeling set up to fail? Feeling manipulated? Nah. It only *feels* like you're getting jerked around like a pork chop at a dogfight!

Seriously, we let the girls know that this is one of those drives-guys-nuts behaviors. And they agreed it's immature and sometimes hurtful. But they also acknowledged they can't seem to help themselves. Sometimes, in fact, they're not even aware of what they're doing until later.

Something powerful deep inside a girl wonders, *Does he really care about me like he says he does?* And so when she subconsciously does things to push him away, she's really hoping he'll hang in there. Because seeing his perseverance is one of the clearest ways she can be reassured that he really does care about her. Learn this now, and you'll develop a skill that will help to minimize these drives-guys-nuts behaviors down the road.

One girl's note to us is a perfect example of what we're talking about:

> Danny was the first guy who could handle me...the good, the bad, and the ugly. He didn't run when he saw my crazy emotions, and as soon as I saw that he was committed, I settled down and the emotions weren't so crazy.

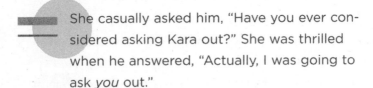

She casually asked him, "Have you ever considered asking Kara out?" She was thrilled when he answered, "Actually, I was going to ask *you* out."

Category 4: hormone poisoning

You knew we were going to get to this. If you've taken health classes or left your cave even once in the past five years, you know that starting at puberty girls endure a biological event roughly every twenty-eight days. Girls say that their menstrual cycle, and the tsunami of hormones that goes with it, is one of the hardest things about being a girl. On those days, at least for some girls, all bets are off.

"ALL I SAID WAS YOU WERE LOOKING A LITTLE PUFFY."

Technically, female hormones aren't poison. Still, we guess there's probably a high correlation between this cycle and unsolved murders and other violence. Your typical victims would be guys dumb enough to make a comment like, "Baby, you puttin' on some weight?"

Guys quickly learn that attaching moodiness or other unexplained behaviors to a girl's period—and actually mentioning that to her—is stupid and dangerous. But since our national survey was done online and you can't actually get decapitated over the Internet, we took the opportunity to do the mentioning for you. Here is what we asked and what the girls said:

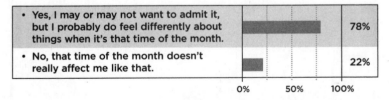

SURVEY Do you sense that when you are at "that time of the month," you sometimes have emotional swings that are out of the ordinary (i.e., you get irritated more easily than normal and you'll be more reasonable in a few days)? (Choose one.)

• Yes, I may or may not want to admit it, but I probably do feel differently about things when it's that time of the month.	78%
• No, that time of the month doesn't really affect me like that.	22%

0%   50%   100%

First, notice that one in five girls doesn't really feel affected by her monthly cycle. That's a huge relief. But also notice that nearly four in five girls do experience out-of-the-ordinary emotional swings—and admit it.

Understandably, most girls you know casually won't tell you they're in PMS mode. What this adds up to for a sensitive guy who hopes for a long life is that you need to keep your antennas up and tuned. We caution you *not* to assume that this is the reason for confusing behavior all the time. After all, PMS isn't an issue most of the month. So it's actually more likely that the reason falls into one of the other categories and you missed it.

But just in case, it's always good to have a plan for how to respond. We'll help you with that in the section that follows.

We guess there's probably a high correlation between this cycle and unsolved murders and other violence.

What to Do When "Random" Strikes

Now that we know that girls are, yes, complicated but not randomly crazy, how should a guy respond? What can a motivated guy say or do when things don't seem quite normal with a girl?

Check out these five commonsense steps for guys who feel like they're stuck in the Twilight Zone with a previously normal girl.

1. Assume there is a reason.

Too many guys shrug off what they don't understand about a girl as, *She's not making sense again,* or, *Must be that time of the month.* Trust us, relationships get unhappy fast when this is as far as a guy is willing to go to understand a person he cares about. But when you see confusing behavior, if you *assume there's a reason and look for it,* you'll be honing a skill that will make both of you much happier.

When you see confusing behavior, if you *assume there's a reason and look for it,* you'll be honing a skill that will make both of you much happier.

2. <u>Remember that feelings are reasons too</u>.

In fact, repeat after us: "Feelings are reasons too. Feelings are reasons too. Feelings…" We guys have to be willing to set aside our old ideas about reality. Girls already know what most guys eventually learn: what you feel is real too. It's just real in a different way. This law of human nature helps us get past the notion that a girl's behavior is random when we don't agree with her perception of what happened or share her feelings.

3. <u>Pay attention. Then if something seems wrong, ask</u>.

Even though "checked out" and "on autopilot" describe how many guys do relationships, it doesn't work. So unless you want to wake up in a relationship ditch, you'd better start paying attention. Think about it. If you don't understand all the systems that make your car run, you don't write off the whole car. Instead you remind yourself that it's more than just a go-cart.

So what to do about that girl? Well, look for signals that something's not quite right. Does she seem distracted or less interested in being around you? Is she upset? Is she not returning your smiles?

Hmm, might be time to...ask. That might sound intimidating, but you'll be reassured by what we found on the survey:

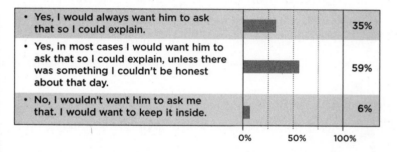

SURVEY Suppose that a guy friend or boyfriend notices that yesterday you were cheerful with him but today you are short with him. Would you want him to approach you and say something like, "I know I may not be the brightest bulb on the tree, but it seems like something's wrong. Can you help me understand what's going on?" (Choose one answer.)

• Yes, I would always want him to ask that so I could explain.	35%
• Yes, in most cases I would want him to ask that so I could explain, unless there was something I couldn't be honest about that day.	59%
• No, I wouldn't want him to ask me that. I would want to keep it inside.	6%

0%   50%   100%

Simply asking, girls say, conveys to them that you care and want to help if you can. In fact, 94 percent of girls said they would like it if a guy asked them sincerely to talk about what's going on. Girls recommend neutral, nonaccusatory, and even funny questions like these:

▸ "I'm not the sharpest knife in the drawer, but it seems like you're upset. Can you help me understand what's going on?"

▸ "Is there anything you want to talk about?"

▸ "If you want to talk about it, I'm here."

All this said, there are two advanced secrets to be aware of at this point, for two different stages of a relationship.

If you're just friends, make it clear that you're available, but don't apply too much pressure. That way if she doesn't want to talk because it would embarrass her or hurt you (four out of five girls said this is sometimes the case), she doesn't have to.

However, if you are officially a couple, remember that if something is wrong in paradise, it is often important to press forward. One girl spoke for many when she wrote this advice: "Accept that a girl will oftentimes say the opposite of what she wants. When we answer 'What's wrong?' with 'Nothing,' it usually means 'Keep asking me until I tell you what's wrong so I know you actually care.'"

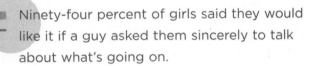

Ninety-four percent of girls said they would like it if a guy asked them sincerely to talk about what's going on.

4. Don't embarrass her.

No matter how weird she's acting, don't make fun of her, especially regarding anything to do with her mood or appearance. For some reason, guys can accomplish stupendous feats of stupidity on this score. Listen to a horror story we heard from Jamie, a high-school senior:

> Recently I've gotten to know this guy in my youth group, Ryan, and I really like him. But I'm also really upset with him right now. Because of a car accident I was in, I've

had a lot of dental work, and at the last youth group meeting, I lost a crown on one of my bottom front teeth. I was so embarrassed! But thankfully I saved the crown, put it in my purse, and tried to keep my mouth shut for the remainder of the meeting.

I didn't talk for a while, and Ryan thought I was mad at him. After a few minutes though, I forgot and started talking. He saw my now weird-looking smile and immediately said, "Hey, open your mouth!"

Oh no! I quickly turned away. He came closer, so I whispered, "I've lost a crown."

"Wow, that looks different. Tom! Come and see this!"

I thought I would die. After all, this was the same guy who had just shared his own insecurities at the last pool party. He had told me he was embarrassed about how his chest was shaped, so he always wore a T-shirt. He had also talked about how he feared losing his hair because of the male pattern baldness that ran in his family. I had totally comforted and encouraged him about those issues and had made a point to build him up in every area. How could this guy with his own insecurities be so insensitive to mine?

Jamie had a plea that we heard from more than one of the girls we interviewed: "Please teach the guys how to be sensitive to girls, especially about their moods and bodies. If a guy is an insensitive clod, it will be hard to trust him and move forward in any kind of close relationship."

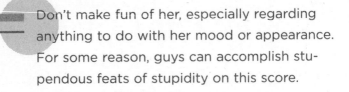

Don't make fun of her, especially regarding anything to do with her mood or appearance. For some reason, guys can accomplish stupendous feats of stupidity on this score.

5. Never ask her if she's on her period. And don't get defensive if she is.

This little piece of advice is so simple you'll be tempted to forget it. Don't.

The only exception is when you have known the girl a long time, are very close friends or dating, and *she has told you in advance that you can ask.* For example, one girl, Cassie, told her boyfriend that if she seemed unusually unreasonable, he could ask her if her evil PMS-ing twin was present: "Um, am I talking to Cassie here or Helga?"

In general, most of the girls we talked to say they really appreciate guys who avoid getting irritated or defensive when she's "under the influence" and just roll with the reality. As one girl explained it:

At that time of the month, the guy I'm dating just doesn't understand that I sometimes don't feel like going out. I feel fat and pale, and I'm worried that something might show. I just want to pull my hair into a ponytail, pull on some old sweatpants, and go eat ice cream with my girl-friends. The last thing I want to do is cuddle with a guy. He gets so offended because he can't relate. But it's just the way things are.

Cassie told her boyfriend that if she seemed unusually unreasonable, he could ask her if her evil PMSing twin was present: "Um, am I talking to Cassie here or Helga?"

6. If all else fails, politely excuse yourself and try again later.

When my (Eric's) daughter Sarah was ten years old, one of her best friends was next-door neighbor John. One day when he was over, Sarah put on a smile, fluttered her eyelids, and asked John a no-win question. "John, who do you think is more beautiful: your sister, your mom, or...me?"

John sat wide-eyed for one beat, said, "Uh, I'll be back later," turned on his heel, and left. The wisdom he showed has become legendary in our family, and now "doing a John" means politely leaving a no-win situation.

Have you sincerely tried the above steps and things keep getting more impossible by the minute? Maybe she's letting the brunt of her unhappiness out on the person in her life she thinks is the safest—you. But sticking around to take it doesn't help her or you. In some cases there just isn't a right way to say something or answer a question.

It might be time for you to do a John. But so that you don't make things worse (and trigger that insecurity we talked about), remember to excuse yourself *and* promise to check back later.

Maybe in a couple of days.

So that you don't make things worse (and trigger that insecurity we talked about), remember to excuse yourself *and* promise to check back later.

Walking with Confidence

So there you have it. We hope you're feeling a little more reassured that girls aren't as random as you originally thought—and that a guy who pays attention and cares can crack the code of their behavior that was confusing before.

Back to our war analogy—every good soldier knows that a land mine is something to be feared only if you don't know where it is buried. But now that you have a few tools to crack the girl code (note that we didn't extend the war analogy to call girls "the enemy" since we think they really are pretty cool), you can walk with confidence through the unknowns and confusing points of your relationships, knowing you don't have to get blown to pieces.

Although…um…it's still a good idea to walk a bit carefully at times.

BREAKING UP, BREAKING YOU

Why girls go from "love" to "get lost" so fast—and how to keep from getting crushed

Toward the end of my first year in college, I (Eric) met Ashley, a cute girl from Memphis, Tennessee, who was shy but gave off vibes that she liked me. We did group dates, a movie here and there, a meal or two, and she smiled a lot at my silly humor. Somehow I got it in my head that she *really* liked me and that a beautiful romance was about to bloom. Summer came, I went back to my small town in Texas, and she went back to Memphis. As the lonely summer set in, I wrote and called as much as possible.

A typical phone conversation went like this:

Eric: Howz things in Memphis? Is it hot?

Ashley: Yes. Muggy too.

Eric: Same here. Um. Uh. How's your job at Applebee's going?

Ashley: Okay. I made twenty dollars in tips last night. (Long pause.)

Eric: Hey, I was thinking about, um, coming to Memphis to see you. (Sweat beading on my forehead.)

Ashley: (Longer pause.) Really? (Another pause.) That might be nice.

Note: If a girl sounds mildly bored, there could be a problem.

Me? I was stoked. So, packing my favorite tunes, I set off on a thirteen-hour drive in the middle of summer in a black car with no air conditioning. (What a guy won't do for a cute girl when she says, "That might be nice.") I occupied my sweltering hours by imagining her running to me as I got out of the car and throwing her arms around my neck.

When I arrived, however, Ashley just said hello and stood there like a post. Her parents greeted me politely, but I figured Ashley was just waiting for them to leave so she could show me how she really felt.

They did, and she did, and it was not what I was hoping for. Basically her point was, "You're a nice guy, Eric, but I don't want to date you."

I wanted to crawl in a hole and die. After a sleepless night in the family guest room, I got back in my hot black car and headed back to Texas. I was hurt and furious. As the long miles and sweaty hours rolled past, I kept thinking, *Why did she lead me on? How could she be so heartless?*

In this chapter we take on that sometimes-miserable game of love every little girl used to play. You know. The one where she shreds a daisy one petal at a time: "He loves me. He loves me not. He loves me. He…" Now that she's all grown up and she's your girlfriend, it feels like she's shredding *you* one piece at a time. She leaves you spinning—or driving back to Texas—with confusing messages. Ever heard her deliver contradictory lines like these, perhaps only days or weeks apart?

- "I really like you."
- "Um, I've got plans."

- "He's so cute" (about you to her girlfriends).
- "Let's just be friends" (about you to you).

- "I'm fine. Really." (She won't look at you.)
- "Couldn't you *tell* something was wrong?!" (She's glaring at you.)

You probably didn't have to drive to Memphis to get rejected by a cute girl. (Save fossil fuel. Get crushed closer to home.) But if it's ever happened to you, or if you have a girlfriend now, we can smell your fear. You know you have no idea what she's really thinking and feeling about you, so you live in dread of the day when another piece of your heart will go missing.

Plenty of guys end up believing that girls are mean, manipulative, heartless wenches. But is that true? We wanted to find out. So we spent a lot of time asking the girls themselves. What they told us was at first so confusing that we just wanted to go back to playing Halo. Or maybe pushing bamboo shoots up under our fingernails.

But we hung in there. You should too. Because what you'll discover will change how you think about girls (well, most girls). With these insights, you'll turn into a genius at reading daisy petals, and we think you'll be more successful at keeping your heart in one piece.

Read this chapter. Read it not. Read this...

Oh, come on. You know you can't resist.

> Plenty of guys end up believing that girls are mean, manipulative, heartless wenches. But is that true?

Meet the Queen of Mean

Before you give up and join a monastery, we have a piece of good news you need to hear—but may not believe. Most girls are not trying to be mean or impossible.

Honest! They told us they do care about a guy's pain and wish it were possible not to hurt him. "No girl wants to be a cutthroat," one girl said. "We don't want to hurt the guy." In fact, most girls insisted that they hated causing a guy pain so much that they would take some of his pain on themselves if they could.

Don't believe us? Here's the first question we asked girls about this subject:

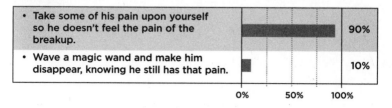

SURVEY Suppose you are breaking up with a nice guy that you've been dating for some time. If you had to choose, which would you do? (Choose one answer.)

• Take some of his pain upon yourself so he doesn't feel the pain of the breakup.	90%
• Wave a magic wand and make him disappear, knowing he still has that pain.	10%

0%   50%   100%

As you can see, nine out of ten girls, given the option, would want to hurt more themselves if that allowed you to hurt less. As one put it, "Of course I'd share the pain if I could! I'm not heartless. I just want to move on." So unless nine out of ten girls are lying, the Queen of Mean is a myth.

But you're no dummy.

"So, Jeff and Eric," you say, hugging your bulletproof vest, "if girls are so nicey-nice, why do we keep taking surprise hits from our 'nice' girlfriends?"

Your question takes us to the big idea of this chapter. And we think it's good news for all guys injured in action. Here it is in a nutshell.

Based on our findings, we propose that most girls are not cold-blooded heartbreakers. In fact, most girls do everything possible to manage the relationship for the least pain. Unfortunately, because girls and guys do relationships so differently, misery still happens. You just think you're playing from the same playbook. But as it turns out, you're not. How guys and girls think, feel, and communicate about their relationships is so different that we might just as well be different species.

Do you think we're kidding? Well, here's something to chew on...

 Most girls do everything possible to manage the relationship for the least pain.

She Loves You, She Dumps You (Wassup, Dog?)

You, dear friend, are a dog. When you get hungry, you find something—anything—to chew on. When you get an itch, you scratch it. When Johnny throws a stinky tennis ball, you fetch it. The sun comes out, you nap. The neighbor's stupid cat walks by, you chase it to Fort Worth.

Guys are like that. For us, life is simple. Life is good.

When it comes to love, we think simple too. Want Cute Girl? Chase Cute Girl. Catch Cute Girl. Do tricks for Cute Girl. Try to kiss Cute Girl.

See what we mean? Love is simple. Love is good.

Girls, though, are not like us. Not at all. What they want from a boyfriend, and how they go about getting it, is entirely different from how males approach the same need. In fact, from the time a girl first smiles at you until she drops you into the recycling bin, she's on a complicated journey. Why she's doing what she's doing or where she wants to go next in the relationship is mostly lost on you. Why? 'Cause of that dog thing. You already caught the girl, the sun is out, and now you have to go catch a Frisbee.

Journey? What journey?

We're exaggerating only slightly. Putting together what the girls in our survey told us, we mapped out a five-stage inner journey that girls travel in a boyfriend relationship. If you look carefully at these five stages, you'll see something scary. You'll realize that you and she are having the same relationship at only two points: at stage 1 and at stage 5.

Stage 5, by the way, is when you get dropped like a bad habit.

Stage 1: She's warm and nice to you; you're happy.

You know what this feels like. At least we hope you do. After a few fun flirtations, you both realize there's something special between you. Or there could be. You decide to spend more time together. Before long, you decide you're a twosome; no other "special" relationships allowed. She's happy and you're happy. You're both in the same zone, feeling the same vibe, speaking the same language.

How could life be this good?

And then your happy twosome gets to stage 2. Well, you don't, but she does.

Stage 2: She's nice but cool; you're happy.

At least half the males in the world never notice stage 2. They're still happy and thinking they are in stage 1, and—like we said—they *caught* the girl. What could go wrong? (Anybody got a doggy treat?)

But having a relationship requires ongoing maintenance, and something you are doing—or not doing—isn't working for her. Maybe it's all that scratching and stinky-ball chasing. Maybe she's not sure what she's unhappy about, but something's bothering her.

So she retreats a little. Cools off a little. Doesn't sound quite so excited when you call. What's happening inside her? She likes you, but she wishes something would change or maybe slow down. Most of the time, she's not being mean. She's just trying to change things in the relationship for the better. She's trying to send you a signal that action on your part is required.*

But what if nothing changes?

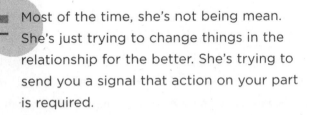

> Most of the time, she's not being mean. She's just trying to change things in the relationship for the better. She's trying to send you a signal that action on your part is required.

---

* Blasts of arctic air can also be a signal when a guy and girl are just friends. A girl will sometimes begin to treat a guy coldly if she senses that he's more interested in her than she is in him. She's not being mean. She's actually trying to spare him the pain of getting his hopes up only to have them dashed.

Stage 3: She's not happy; you're probably still happy.

She's not happy now. She really wants the relationship to change. Or she wants out. So she's sending up a nearly constant stream of danger flares. She wants you to know that a new ice age is around the corner. But if you're like most guys, you're probably still clueless.

Why? Because she's signaling you *indirectly*. Don't know what "indirect" looks like? Girls gave us some examples:

- She gets upset or annoyed more easily.
- She says, "You're not listening," a lot.
- She becomes less available.
- She makes excuses to go home early.

You figure she's just more complicated than you expected. Or moodier. But more than likely she's trying to tell you something important.

A girl finds it hard to be straightforward about her feelings. In large part that's because she's sensitive and doesn't want to hurt you. This is especially true if she doesn't like being with you as much as she did or if she wants out. So she'll hem and haw and won't be straightforward about things. Meanwhile, you're running around the yard, happily chasing your tail.

One girl told us, "Months before I actually break up with you, I'm getting over you. You just haven't picked up on my clues."

If indirect signals don't work, girls move on to stage 4.

> "Months before I actually break up with you, I'm getting over you. You just haven't picked up on my clues."

Stage 4: She's not nice; now you're not happy.

At this point she figures the relationship probably isn't going to work. Why would it? To her, you seem clueless and unwilling to change. You'd think at this point she'd actually *tell* you what's wrong and what she wants. But no. What happens next, girls told us, is that she'll start being difficult, maybe impossible. She'll treat you badly.

Is that because she's finally turned into the Queen of Mean? The answer still is no, insisted our sources. She's simply trying to get you

so irritated that *you* will be the one to break up with *her,* or at least you won't be as sad once she does.

Did you get that flow of logic, Rover? She treats you like a bad stink for no reason that you can see = She is just trying to get you to notice a problem = She is a nice person who cares about your future. (Where did we put those bamboo shoots?)

> She's trying to get you so irritated that you will be the one to break up with her.

One college girl told us, "I personally will start trying to be annoying so that he's not as sad about it—so that when we do come to the breakup, *he* thinks it's for the best. A girl will give him the cold shoulder so he doesn't like her as much. And that makes the breakup easier on everyone. But that's probably what the guys are perceiving as mean."

No, really. Ya think?

Stage 5: She dumps you; you're shocked—and not at all happy.

Think about the last few times you got that punched-in-the-gut feeling with a girl. Did you, by any chance, see a pattern leading up to it? You may not have, since we guys aren't good at picking up the subtle clues girls use. Unfortunately for many of us guys, we only start reading these signs after a girl has already reached the Point of No Turning Back in her mind.

Imagine a guy-girl relationship as a party for two on the deck of a lovely cruise ship (let's say it's the *Titanic*). The guy is just enjoying the party. The girl? She's been noticing icebergs to the left and to the right for days—and trying to get you to notice too!

Suddenly there's a big crash, and your love boat starts to sink. But the only person on deck who is surprised is…you.

Get the picture? Girls say they continually send guys signals when something is wrong. But most guys miss all of them. Then one day—*wham!*

Here's what one girl told us:

When I break up with a guy, it might seem abrupt or cruel. But I've typically been thinking about it for months. I've been waiting for him to change in some areas, and I get more and more detached if he doesn't. Once a girl is detached, *then* she can break up. By the time she's able to do that, she's cried all her tears and has already checked out.

Now you see how a guy can go from "She's warm and nice" to "I've been dumped; she's so cold!" without knowing what happened. But it doesn't have to be that way. That's what we want to talk about next.

For many of us guys, we only start reading these signs after a girl has already reached the Point of No Turning Back in her mind.

Turning the *Titanic* Before Hitting the Iceberg

Ashley *had* given me (Eric) about a dozen clues that I should have seen, but I was too bullheaded and pushy to recognize them. I was steaming full speed ahead through increasingly frigid waters, ignoring the possibility of an iceberg ahead. I hate to say this, but it was my own fault that my heart got smashed into pieces.

What we found from our interviews is that if a guy pays attention to what the girl is really saying—with her actions as well as her words—and responds accordingly, the story can easily turn out much more happily for everyone. Look closely at what the girls said about this on our national survey:

SURVEY Suppose you've been dating a guy for quite some time. You've seen him in all different situations, enjoy each other's company, and have discovered that you're very compatible. Suppose that sometime later you start thinking about breaking up with him. Of the following reasons why you might be considering that, what do you think would be the most likely one? (Choose one answer.)

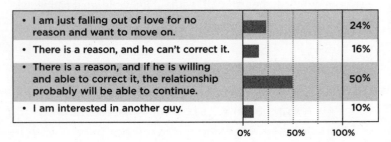

• I am just falling out of love for no reason and want to move on.	24%
• There is a reason, and he can't correct it.	16%
• There is a reason, and if he is willing and able to correct it, the relationship probably will be able to continue.	50%
• I am interested in another guy.	10%

0%   50%   100%

Notice that two out of every three girls said that there is some-thing specific going on that is making them want to break up. For the guy, it may seem like the breakup comes from out of the blue. But for the girl, there's a specific reason. Only one in four girls said they fall out of love for no reason.

Now notice that half of all the girls said that even after they started thinking about breaking up, the situation wasn't totally lost. Those girls said that if the guy were willing and able to correct the problem, the relationship probably would be able to continue. We think that the number would be much higher in situations where the girl hadn't already gotten to the point of considering a breakup—dur-ing the phase when she was wishing and hoping that he would see her unhappiness and correct whatever was hurting or disappointing her.

> Half of all the girls said that even after they started thinking about breaking up, the situation wasn't totally lost.

During an interview with one girl, we asked what would happen if a guy saw the signals that something was wrong (for example, that she was more stressed than usual) and did something sweet or nice for her. The girl smiled. "If she really does like him," she said, "she'll jump at that and be thrilled. Of course, if there is some problem that he isn't fixing—like he keeps flirting with her best friend—then tak-ing her to a meal or movie isn't going to fix it. He needs to be willing to address the actual issue instead of trying to avoid it."

Now is a good time to loop back and pay more attention to those iceberg-ahead signals we missed the first time around.

A Guy's Guide to Reading the Signals

On behalf of every confused guy out there, we asked girls how guys could tell that something was wrong in a relationship. How can a guy know that his girl is checking out emotionally and he's about to find himself sinking to the bottom of the icy Atlantic?

The girls were willing to tell us what some of their "I'm unhappy with you" or "I'm thinking about getting out of this relationship" hints are. The list that follows starts with the signals girls say they send when things can still be fixed. The farther down the list you go, the more likely the signal means the relationship is doomed. We asked them to complete this sentence: "If I'm checking out of the relationship, I usually…"

- act less bubbly (Iceberg sighted!)
- act less affectionate
- stop asking him questions about his life (The sailors run to warn the bridge.)
- start reminiscing about the past instead of enjoying the present
- seem sad or distracted (You've hit the iceberg and are taking on water.)
- get upset or annoyed more easily (Your radio man begins sending out an SOS.)

- say, "You're not listening," a lot (Bulkheads are collapsing noisily.)
- become less available (The bow begins to go under.)
- make excuses to go home early
- act less excited when he calls—and stop calling him
- start bickering ("All souls to the lifeboats!")
- cut conversations short (Not enough room in the lifeboats!)
- start criticizing (Grab a lifejacket.)
- start controlling (Jump into the icy water.)
- say disrespectful things
- defy his wishes, not letting him lead (You can't feel your legs.)
- put him down in front of others (You're curiously looking up at ice floating above you.)

Spend some time reviewing this list so you won't be clueless in the future. Remember, the closer to the top of that list, the more the signals are likely to mean that something needs to be talked about or changed *and there's still time to save your ship.*

Do you recognize any of this behavior from a past or present girlfriend relationship? If so, what was (or what could be) your response? Guys who know how to read the signs don't have to be clueless and won't need to experience that "I can't believe I just got dumped" feeling.

Guys who know how to read the signs won't need to experience that "I can't believe I just got dumped" feeling.

Clueless No More

Let's assume that the just-got-dumped feeling is *not* on your list of favorite things in life. What could you take away from this chapter that might help you avoid that special experience?

1. Pay attention.

We've given you a list of signals. But paying attention begins with your willingness to care, to believe there could be trouble in paradise, and to listen. One girl told us, "A lot of the problem stems from guys just not listening and hearing what we're trying to say. I've talked to lots of my girlfriends about this, and every one of them says the same thing."

If you can't figure out what the problem might be, then simply ask. Something like, "Hey, Emily, I'm getting a feeling that something just isn't right between us. Is there something that I'm doing or maybe not doing that is bugging you?"

Don't just hope her mood will blow over. Often, when you see signs of trouble, you only have a little time to turn things around. What she sees may be an iceberg dead ahead.

2. React calmly.

Guys are notorious for getting offended and overreacting to their girlfriend's slightest criticisms or suggestions. This behavior is dumb and immature, it prompted complaints from the majority of girls, and it is one of the main reasons girls revert to subtle, easy-to-miss signals—because they've learned that we overreact to the big ones. Nine out of ten confirmed that this is why they aren't as direct as guys might want them to be.

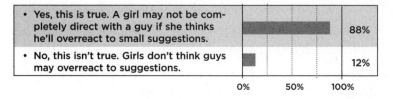

SURVEY Do you think this statement is true or false? "Sometimes, when a girl wants a guy to change something, she is only suggesting small adjustments on his part but doesn't end up being direct with him because she thinks he might overreact." (Choose one answer.)

• Yes, this is true. A girl may not be completely direct with a guy if she thinks he'll overreact to small suggestions.	88%
• No, this isn't true. Girls don't think guys may overreact to suggestions.	12%

0%   50%   100%

A girl wants to know she can be honest with her guy, especially if what she's looking for is a minor change. In chapter 4 we told the story of Jessie and Rob sitting on the couch. Jessie pushed Rob's arm away because she spotted her mom outside the window doing her gardening. What we didn't mention is that Rob proceeded to move to the other end of the couch and stay there for the next hour. Jessie was totally annoyed. She wanted just a small adjustment ("Let's not sit with your arm draped over me when my folks can see us; it makes me feel weird"). But instead she got a huge adjustment, as Rob added three feet of space between them. Jessie told us, "It makes me feel like I can never bring up something that's bugging me, because he's going to flip out."

It takes courage for a girl to be honest. So respect her courage, listen, and save the drama for the next school play.

Girls revert to subtle, easy-to-miss signals because they've learned that we overreact to the big ones.

3. If there's a problem, fix it if you can.

Once you understand what's bothering her, take action if you can. If she's feeling insecure about whether you care about her, reassure her. If she says you don't listen, you can learn. (See chapter 6 for tips.) Sometimes all it takes to keep her from checking out emotionally is to simply make it clear that you *want* to understand and address the issue.*

4. If you've blown it, apologize and try to make things right.

We all do and say things that hurt those we care about. That's why knowing how to sincerely say you're sorry and show you care is so important.

And if you've *really* blown it, don't expect the first apology to necessarily get through and make everything perfect again. It takes

---

* Of course, if she's a cavernous vacuum of neediness or a chronic criticizer, you can't fix that. But if she has seemed like a relatively normal person up to this point, it's worth making an effort.

guts to keep pursuing a girl until she is really able to hear you apologize. But persevering is important. Own your part of the problem. And make a real apology, not a fake one ("If you perceived that I possibly did something wrong..."). After you're sure she's really heard you *and* you have made it clear that you want things to move forward, it's up to her.

5. Be willing to move on.

If you've tried to fix whatever you can in the relationship and you realize it's over, do what every guy has had to do at some time in his life (probably even your dad, about a hundred years ago): move on. Your parents may be telling you the exact same thing, and it's worth listening. This is definitely one of those areas where it helps to have the perspective of a few extra years.

Anyway, you did your best, and you'll do better next time. What might seem like an unmitigated tragedy (that means it *really* hurts) now will turn out for the best in the long run. Trust us on this one!

Many guys are mystified because so many girls break up with guys and say things like, "But I still care for you." This often gives us hope, and we keep pursuing the girl—only to get our hearts broken again. Can you relate? Why on earth would she break up with me and then add, "But I still care about you"? We're like the guy in *Dumb & Dumber* who, when the girl of his dreams said there was only a one in a million chance for them to be together, exclaimed, "So you're tellin' me there's a chance!"

Which brings us to our last survey-based advice in this chapter:

don't assume that her "care" for you is equivalent to romantic feelings. This is just her sensitivity causing you a lot of trouble again. Girls assured us that the statement means exactly what it says and no more. On our survey, we asked girls this question:

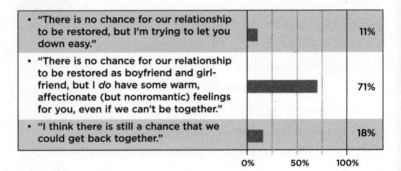

SURVEY If you were to break up with a boyfriend and say to him, "But I still care for you," what does that most likely mean? (Choose one answer.)

• "There is no chance for our relationship to be restored, but I'm trying to let you down easy."	11%
• "There is no chance for our relationship to be restored as boyfriend and girl-friend, but I *do* have some warm, affectionate (but nonromantic) feelings for you, even if we can't be together."	71%
• "I think there is still a chance that we could get back together."	18%

0%   50%   100%

Don't miss the facts here. Even when a girl says, "I still care for you," she believes that there's no chance for the relationship to be restored. Only one in five girls on the survey said that would even be an option.

We're like the guy in *Dumb & Dumber* who, when the girl of his dreams said there was only a one in a million chance for them to be together, exclaimed, "So you're tellin' me there's a chance!"

Real Love Is When...

In this chapter and the previous one, we've looked at how girls communicate when they need more attention or care from you.

Now, some cynical people think teenage guys are only out for one thing and don't care what girls need from them. But we think you *do* care. Sure, most of us have a tendency to focus on the short term. And all of us guys have a tendency to be paralyzed by the thought that we've failed someone important to us. But we also believe that God has built into every guy a desire to protect and encourage girls.

You see, despite what we said earlier, you're not really a dog. Now that you know how girls act when they feel uncertain or unhappy, you don't have to be a clueless slave to instinct. You can wake up to ways you can put your God-given gifts into action. You can be the kind of guy who tries to outdo his girl in giving, understanding, and respecting.

People don't often say "get lost" to that kind of guy.

NO DROPPED CALLS

How to talk and listen to a girl without looking like an idiot

I (Jeff) remember a date with a girl that started off like the Fourth of July—lights, color, action. I was putting on one impressive show. Then suddenly it fizzled, and I felt very stupid. The evening shouldn't have ended that way, but it did.

If I tell you about it, will you try to figure out where I went wrong? Here goes.

Anna was a cute little blonde who sat next to me in World History. We had so much in common. Anna liked high school; so did I. She breathed air; so did I. She performed ballet; I played football. She loved PBS; I loved shows with bad people doing bad things, especially if it involved bullets.

Okay, maybe we didn't have *everything* in common.

Leading up to the date, I was pretty nervous. What were we going to talk about? It helped that she was cute, but still! I figured all I could do was prepare ahead, so I dreamed up multiple topics of conversation. Then I stood in front of my bedroom mirror and nervously practiced what I was going to say on each topic. That helped. But you know that old trick from speech class where they say it helps you relax if you imagine your audience in their underwear? That didn't help with Anna. No, it did not.

I kept practicing. But the closer we got to the date, the more I kept hearing a separate conversation running through my head telling me, *Jeff, just don't screw up. What a dumb thing to say! She can so tell that you're scared to death. Oh man, I wish this was over!*

But, like I said, our actual date started beautifully. I moved from one rehearsed topic to the next. Fireworks were going off everywhere. I was magnificent! Then it happened…

I ran out of material. I was driving in the car, the cute girl I'd been thinking about for months sitting beside me, and my mind was mush. I had nothing to say. All my *blah blah blah* had gone blank—and we were left with awkward silence.

Minutes passed. I was desperate, racking my brain, but nothing came. Finally I blurted out, "Well, I don't have anything to say," and I looked over at her.

I'll never forget the look on Anna's face. Come to think of it, she may have had that look on her face during my entire performance. I don't know because I hadn't really looked at her. But the look on her face at that moment was…not good. She was staring at me open-mouthed, like I had two heads.

Chalk up another one for Mr. Smooth.

What could I have done differently? How could I have not run out of things to say? In fact, how does a guy communicate with a girl *at all* without making a complete idiot out of himself?

In this chapter we deliver valuable tips for guys—and some equally valuable encouragement. For starters, girls insist that approaching them and talking to them doesn't require days of preparation in front of a mirror. As a matter of fact, the only thing it does require is letting them know you're interested in what *they* have to say. Here's what the girls told us.

> Girls insist that approaching them and talking to them doesn't require days of preparation.

Talk with Your Ears; Listen with Your Heart

Write this down: *The way to a girl's heart is through your ears.* That's why we say, "Talk with your ears." And that means listen first. Then, after you've heard her words, listen carefully to her feelings.

Did you notice that this statement actually says nothing about how to talk? We're doing that on purpose. Of course, real communication is about both talking *and* listening. Problem is, most of us guys tie ourselves up in knots trying to be good talkers, but we don't think much about being good listeners. So in this chapter we'll download some practical points about listening as well as talking.

And speaking of talking, the girls passed along some great news. They are much more approachable and easier to talk to—and impress—than we ever thought. They *want* a guy to give it a shot. And get this: when we nervously stammer and stumble around, we can come off as more appealing, even (the girls said) "cute."

Okay, this is *really* not what we think! But the girls insist it's true. They are very attracted to a guy with confidence, yes. But remember the "Average Joe" chapter? Your confidence is evident in your willingness to approach a girl even when you're nervous. Look at the proof from our national survey:

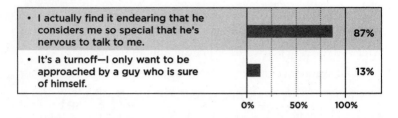

SURVEY Suppose a guy comes up and wants to initiate a conversation with you. He seems like a nice guy, but he also seems shy or uncertain how to approach you.

Which of the following are you most likely to be thinking? (Choose one.)

• I actually find it endearing that he considers me so special that he's nervous to talk to me.	87%
• It's a turnoff—I only want to be approached by a guy who is sure of himself.	13%

0%   50%   100%

Did you see that? Almost nine out of ten girls said that, instead of being turned off, they would actually like it if they felt a guy cared enough to try to communicate, even if he wasn't confident about how to do it.

▸ "I think it's sweet when a guy stutters a little or looks just a little nervous when he's approaching me. It makes me feel I'm a prize worth the effort."

▸ "When this hot guy at my school stuttered and got embarrassed when he was talking to me, I thought it was so cool because I knew then that he wasn't some smooth, experienced ladies' man."

▸ "I feel like most girls aren't really as mean as guys think they would be. It doesn't dissuade me at all when a guy is a little timid. He just has to be willing to hold a conversation."

Bottom line? If we stop sweating so much about talking, and if we start practicing our listening skills even if we lack confidence, we'll be fine. Because the Anna in your life doesn't want or expect you to perform. She's just hoping to meet the real you. Now for those practical how-tos.

> "I think it's sweet when a guy stutters a little or looks just a little nervous when he's approaching me."

A Talking and Listening Cheat Sheet for Hearing-Impaired Males

Just because communication skills don't come naturally for most young guys doesn't mean you can't make rapid progress with the help of a decent cheat sheet. Here's ours.

1. Relax. Don't spew.

Don't get offended, but most people tend to look smarter when they keep their mouth closed. That bit of wisdom is even biblical: "Even a fool is thought wise if he keeps silent, and discerning if he holds his tongue." We're not saying that you should turn into a stump or, if you're already the shyest guy in class, that you shouldn't try to talk. But endlessly saying anything that pops into your brain, especially about yourself, is not a conversation. Not even with a stump. Girls said things like this:

> ▸ "If guys are always talking about themselves, they won't show interest in your life."
>
> ▸ "At first you might be attracted, but if he just goes on about himself, it's like, 'Dude, stop talking about yourself!'"

The best thing a guy can do, girls advised, is to forget the whole performance mind-set. Instead, just relax and imagine you're goofing around with a friend. Not a date, not a future wife, not the fate of the world. Truth is, your future happiness in life doesn't depend on your saying the funniest or most interesting thing during the first ten minutes you're with a cute girl. And while a little preparation isn't a bad thing if it helps you feel more confident, you don't you have to script everything you want to say. In fact, scripting might add to your stress and make it difficult to adjust to changing conversation topics.

As one girl put it, "Become a girl's best friend first. You are way more likely to have a good relationship." So instead of obsessing about your performance, think ahead about *her*. What does she like to do? What kind of family does she come from? Who does she hang

"COME OVER HERE, GIRL. I'M DOING THIS FOR YOU!"

out with? What experiences, good and bad, do you have in common? These are starting places for a good conversation.

Which leads to the next tip.

Your future happiness in life doesn't depend on your saying the funniest or most interesting thing during the first ten minutes you're with a cute girl.

2. Ask good questions.

Don't know what to say? Get *her* to talk! Some of the best advice on this point comes from a seventy-year-old book called *How to Win Friends and Influence People.* The premise of the book is this: the way to be perceived as a great conversationalist—and have people like you—is to focus on the other person.

My (Eric's) seventeen-year-old daughter said, "I think all guys need to read this book. It will really help them move away from the cocky talking and learn to become good interviewers. They'd get so much further with girls if they would."

Across the board, girls told us they're not looking for you to carry the load in a conversation but rather to ask good questions and tune in to what a girl is trying to tell you about her life. "It would be so great for a guy to learn about us from *us*," one girl said. "It would make such a good impression if he put effort into learning about me."

3. Listen to her answers. (Duh!)

Someone once said, "Be a good listener. Your ears will never get you into trouble." The simple fact is that everyone likes to be heard, and listening is truly the way to a girl's heart. If you learn how to be a good listener, it will make her, the speaker, feel good.

The basics for listening to a girl boil down to ensuring that she

knows you're listening. It sounds simple, and it is. One of the best ways to show that you're giving her your attention is to make eye contact. Okay, if she's the most beautiful girl you've ever stood next to, you might prefer some ancient form of torture rather than looking her in the eye. But try it. You'll see that it works.

One girl said, "There's something about being looked in the eye. It makes me think that the reason he's fascinated is because of what I'm saying. My self-confidence gets a lift by him showing that I'm an interesting person, that my opinion matters."*

---

* Now don't go overboard and think that if a little eye contact is good, a lot must be better. *Yes! I'll stare at her, unblinking, like a puppy in love!* The girls said, "Uh, no. That's just creepy."

Now two other easier tips. First, nod once in a while so she knows you're in receive mode. And second, occasionally react so she knows you're tracking with her. For example, "Kara said that to you? Really?" or, "I'll bet that wasn't fun."

One girl summed it up this way: "Good listening is just politeness, and I want a guy who's polite. Actually, I want a good southern boy because their mamas beat them until they find some manners." (This was our favorite comment from all the focus groups. We almost spewed our sodas.)

 Be a good listener. Your ears will never get you into trouble.

4. Listen to the feelings hiding in her words.

Now we've arrived at what you could call advanced listening. Listening for exceptionally brilliant guys who number only a few per million. Listening that will amaze your friends and terrify your foes.

Even though you've asked the good question and you've heard her reply, your job isn't yet done. A girl wants a guy not only to listen to her, as in physically using your ears. She also needs you to listen for the right thing—for how she *feels* about what she has just said.

There's a scene in *Spider-Man 3* that perfectly illustrates this. Mary Jane has seen Peter Parker (you know, Spider-Man) kiss another girl during an awards ceremony. The two are back at Peter's cruddy little apartment, and things aren't going well. Peter has been getting cocky and inattentive, and he has missed every signal Mary Jane has sent him about how unhappy she is. She eventually bursts out with a cry for help. "I just want you to listen to me!" she pleads. "I just need you to *hear how I feel*!"

Can you believe it? Here's Spider-Man, smacking down evil-doers and swinging from skyscrapers. He's idolized by small children and always has the words *The Amazing* come before his name. And that's not good enough for MJ?

No.

Why?

'Cause she's just like every other girl!

No doubt all of Spidey's web slinging and derring-do played a part in attracting MJ to him. But still—write this down too—*she is willing to trade all of that for someone who will really listen to her feelings!* It isn't just about her problem (he kissed another girl) but about how she's feeling about the problem (she's feeling lonely and ready to hand him his Spidey-suited head on a plate).

A lot of guys struggle in this area. We struggle to listen to words period, and we often fail miserably at listening to feelings. Partly because of our brain wiring, we have to be more attentive and purposeful about processing the whole range of feelings when a female is talking so we don't miss them.

My (Eric's) father-in-law is a "just the facts" kind of guy. My wife, Lisa, saw this when she was on her way home from a speaking engagement in Chicago that hadn't turned out the way she'd hoped.

Calling from the airport, she had both her parents on the phone and was lamenting that the audience didn't seem to connect with her.

Her mother jumped in with, "Oh, honey, I can imagine how devastated you must be feeling."

What did Dad say? "Which airport you flying out of? Midway or O'Hare?"

Wrong, wrong, wrong! said the girls we interviewed. They want their feelings to be heard and validated *first*. The "which airport" question comes later. (Actually, maybe never.)

Here's how we put the question to the girls in our survey:

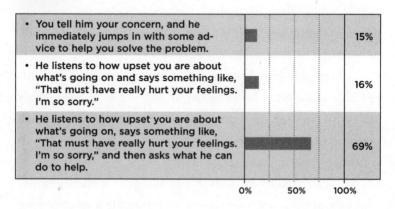

SURVEY Imagine that you're having a problem with a female friend in your class. If you tell your boyfriend about it, what would be the best way for him to handle it? (Choose one answer.)

• You tell him your concern, and he immediately jumps in with some advice to help you solve the problem.	15%
• He listens to how upset you are about what's going on and says something like, "That must have really hurt your feelings. I'm so sorry."	16%
• He listens to how upset you are about what's going on, says something like, "That must have really hurt your feelings. I'm so sorry," and then asks what he can do to help.	69%

0%   50%   100%

A huge majority—85 percent—want a special kind of listening, the kind where the guy is hearing the emotion behind a girl's words.

"We want to be validated for what we're feeling," one college girl told us. "We want him to listen so we know he sincerely cares."

> Partly because of our brain wiring, we have to be more attentive and purposeful about processing the whole range of feelings when a female is talking so we don't miss them.

5. Don't try to fix her.

Did you notice that only a small percentage of girls want the guy to jump in with a fix? The vast majority want the guy to understand their feelings first.

This response feels sick and wrong to an honest man. Like putting on your shoes, then your socks. Men just do things differently.

Say your buddy Danny has a problem and he's getting emotional. You know what happens: you *interrupt* his outburst so you can fix his problem. "Danny! Hey!" you say as you turn onto the on ramp. "It's just a flippin' double-patty-with-extra-bacon cheeseburger! We'll make sure they get the extra bacon in there tomorrow, okay?"

Done. Danny fixed.

Unfortunately, this isn't a winning technique with girls.

We know you're thinking, *Why would you tell someone about a problem if you didn't want advice about solving the problem?* Most guys feel that way, but most girls don't. And it's not that the girls don't necessarily want a fix *at all*. They just don't want it *first*. First they want you to pay attention to all those emotions you'd rather be done with. After you have shared their pain, *then* they'll be much more able to hear your brilliant ideas for solving their problem.

Since we're concerned with how the girls feel about this issue (because we're not interested in taking a *guy* to the prom), we need to pay attention. You see, to the girl, her real problem is actually a different problem from what you thought. If she were in Danny's place, her problem would not be the problem itself ("Hey! Where's my extra bacon?"). It would be how she *feels* about the missing extra bacon ("I just feel so angry and ripped off and...*sob*...disappointed!").

One girl said, "We really aren't looking for a big analysis or even the answer. We just want to know that our feelings about the situation count for something."

So let's practice. When a girl tells you about a problem she's having, you need to put on your detective hat and figure out what she's really struggling with. Here's another situation: Supercompetitive Simona texts you. "UGH!" she writes. "Coach Harding is BUGGING me to play basketball this season, and I can't get him off my back!"

What should you say in reply to Simona? Choose one:

1. "LOL. Wanna get some CHICKEN wings?"
2. "EZY. Tell him your decision is final. UR not playing."
3. "H8 that kind of pressure!!! But you were stellar last season. What's making you feel so UGH! this year?"

If you chose 1, slap yourself and start reading this chapter again from the top.

If you chose 2, refocus and read the previous two sections again, starting with "4. Listen to the feelings hiding in her words."

If you chose 3, congratulations! You get to advance to the next level. P.S. Simona wants to go out with you.

> To the girl, her real problem is actually a
> different problem from what you thought.

6. Finally...you're ready to talk.

Conversation is how people get closer, especially if one of them is a girl. Sure, you and your buddy Danny get close just by doing stuff— turning out for sports, watching sports, eating burgers. Throw in a few grunts, and you're lifelong friends. But for girls, actual conversation is huge.

Surely you realize by now that at no point in my (Jeff's) Fourth of July speeches during my date with Anna was a conversation actually happening. That's because I was a talking parrot—no listener required. I should have just e-mailed her the MP3 file and stayed home.

So when we say *talking* in this section, we're not thinking speeches or parrots or recordings. We mean conversation—real get-to-know-you skills that work for two people interested in each other.

As one girl told us, "If guys will learn to listen by asking good questions, they'll suddenly find themselves with a lot of friends— including girls."

Here are a few pointers and reminders:

- Become a good interviewer and listen to her answers. If you want someone to be intrigued by you and to think you are an incredible conversationalist, don't talk about yourself—talk about her. When you're with a girl, ask her questions about herself.

- Dump questions that invite a yes or no response. The answers don't go anywhere, and the other person will stop talking. "Do you have brothers?" isn't as good as, "What's your family like?" Use questions that encourage her to describe something or tell a story or share an opinion or feeling. The girls we interviewed guaranteed that almost any girl will leave that sort of conversation thinking, *Wow!*

- Use follow-up questions. For example, when she tells you about her family, let's say she mentions how much it stinks to share a bedroom or have a stepmom. Now you can follow up on two things related to the topic of her family. Go for it.

- Don't fake it. Girls are smart. Let's just get that out in the open. She can tell if you're doing something just to get in good with her, not because you're interested and actually care.

- Avoid overkill. This usually happens when guys aren't sure what to say, so we go way over the top. Like saying, "How did that make you feel?" a dozen times in a row or at the wrong time.

Her: "I skipped lunch yesterday."

You: "How did that make you feel?"

Oh boy.

Another form of overkill is nonstop running at the mouth, like, "You look so beautiful, Rachel. Your hair looks a little lighter today, Rachel. Did you lighten it? Have you been working out? Are other people in your family big boned?"

You'll get slugged. Trust us.

Good Effort, Good Times

We know there aren't many places in this world where sincerity and good intentions matter for much. In business and sports, nobody says, "Aw, that was a good try, Bob. Sure, you lost the big one for our team. But your heart was in the right place."

With girls, it's different. Honestly. They like guys who try way more than they like guys who are perfect. Look at these two great comments:

▸ "I know guys get scared about communicating with girls, but we're not expecting perfection—just like we hope they're not expecting it from us."

▸ "We want a guy to talk to us or ask us out, even if it's not perfectly smooth. We'll respect him more, not less, if he's himself and is trying for us. It's sweet and charming."

It seems that girls are more able to accept us guys as works in progress and see the potential in us even when we don't. That's why, even though communication skills don't come naturally to most of us, we can relax, learn, and keep practicing. Talking with your ears and listening with your heart are powerful life skills that every successful person has to work at sooner or later.

Think about it. Did you learn to catch a ball the first time someone threw it to you? What about skateboarding? Did you learn to grind in a day? Same thing with talking and listening skills.

And since girls are really cute and smell nice, putting out a little effort here is one of the smartest moves you'll ever make.

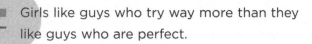

Girls like guys who try way more than they like guys who are perfect.

WHAT IT REALLY MEANS TO SCORE

The truth about girls, guys, and sex

Welcome to the book. You're about to learn what most guys miss…

You're busted, right?

If we just caught you starting the book here, don't feel too bad. We know how it goes. When guys pick up the book, the pages magically turn to this chapter.

You could just keep reading, but you'd miss out on a lot. Why? Because you've jumped into the middle without a beginning. You've stumbled into a battle scene in Warcraft—and you've never even played before. You have no idea what's going on, who you are, who the bad guys are, or even what you're supposed to do to stay alive in Azeroth.

So we strongly recommend that you jump out of this chapter and start at the beginning. The book is a quick read, and what you'll learn about girls will help you stay alive in this chapter. Okay, at least it will set you up to get a lot more out of it. Think of it as saving the best for last—and not missing the best because you got eaten by the Undead while you were standing there saying, "Huh?"

You see, this is a dangerous chapter. The world is a sparky place, sex hormones are highly flammable, and unfortunately you're soaking in them. Just as in every other chapter, you're going to read stuff about girls you've never heard before, stuff you may have a hard time believing. Without the right foundation, you could take what you learn and hurt girls or yourself. You could completely misunderstand what we say.

And we don't want that to happen. So here's your chance to start at the beginning. This chapter will still be here when you get back.

◀ ◀ ◀ ◀ ◀

Before we dive into this chapter, we should provide you with some, um, protection.

▸ *Information is not recommendation.* As with everything else up to this point, just because we're fulfilling our promise to bring you what girls actually said doesn't mean we always endorse it. Some of the girls we talked to had already crossed the line into sex. Others said how they would feel if they did. But please don't think we recommend that you cross the line and become sexually active. We don't.

▸ *To get the truth, we stayed home.* Well, Jeff and Eric did, that is. We asked Shaunti and Lisa to conduct all the focus

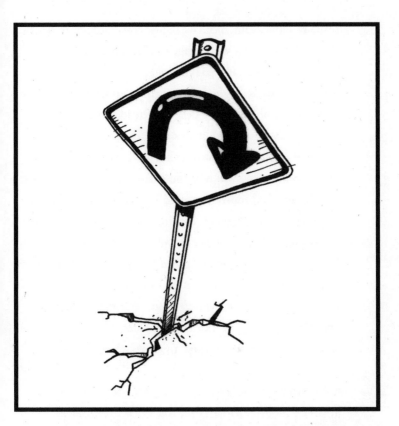

groups and interviews on this subject. (If you don't know who Shaunti and Lisa are, dude, you're still busted: you really need to read the rest of the book first.) We helped our sources get honest by making this an all-girl conversation.

▸ *We didn't talk only to "nice" girls.* As on every other subject, we interviewed and surveyed representative teen girls from across the country—most nice, some probably not; some sexually active, some not. We're just crazy enough to believe that hearing from a wide range of girls makes our report even more helpful and convincing.

▸ *Turns out, God was right.* When it comes to sex in the twenty-first century, not everyone believes that statement, but it's true. If you've grown up in a strong Christian or Jewish family, for example, you know that sex was created for marriage. Yet almost nothing you hear these days agrees with that. We do. (*Whew!* God must be relieved.) In fact, we're enthusiastic about the New Testament teaching that we are to surrender our bodies to God as an act of worship and lifelong service. Interestingly, *everything we learned from girls themselves in this survey confirms all those old-fashioned morals you hear in church or synagogue.* And it turns out, almost everything you hear about teens and sex in movies, magazines, TV, and the hallway at school is horse hockey. You'll see why in a minute.

Everything we learned from girls themselves in this survey confirms all those old-fashioned morals you hear in church or synagogue.

Sex Changes Everything

We got our first window into how girls really feel about "crossing the line" from an early focus group Shaunti and Lisa conducted with college girls, some of whom had already had sex. When Shaunti and Lisa asked them how they felt in the days and months afterward, the comments that came back shocked us:

- ▸ "You feel more attached."
- ▸ "You feel vulnerable, upset, regretful…resentful."
- ▸ "Afterward I wanted to mend things and make the relationship deeper than it really was, so I used the physical aspect to keep him around and fix it and make it better, even though I felt cheapened in the end."
- ▸ "You feel clingy, and you have to keep him there so there won't be a black mark on your record. You don't want it to end with giving part of yourself away and having nothing to show for it."
- ▸ "It puts you in a place of constant fear. You're always asking, *Am I really lovable? Is he satisfied with me?*"

Three things we did *not* hear—not even once—were: (1) "Afterward, I realized what a hunk of burning love my boyfriend is." (2) "I'm really glad I did it. I can't wait to do it again." (3) "Now I respect him *so* much!"

Oh.

At first we wondered if our female subjects were emotional basket cases or maybe alien droids in disguise. But they weren't. Over and over again we heard the same thing from other girls around the country, including on our national survey.

SURVEY If a girl and her partner made the move to a sexual relationship, which of the following thoughts or emotions would she be likely to feel? (Choose all that apply.)

"Positive feelings, such as more love and closeness"	**67%**
• More love and closeness with him	
• More attachment in a loving and free way	
• More trust in him	
• Assurance that this relationship is really working and likely has a future	
• Relief, since she now knows he truly loves her	
"Negative feelings, such as feeling possessive, insecure, or clingy"	**82%**
• Worried about losing him / losing the relationship the way it was	
• Concerned about what he might be telling others	
• Exposed, vulnerable	
• More attachment to him in a possessive way	
• Possessive and wanting to keep tabs on him	
• Regretful	
• Like she's made a mistake and now she has to fix it	
• That he now owes her something (like greater commitment, loyalty, "reporting in" on where he is and what he's doing, etc.)	
• More controlling, like she needs to make sure he treats her right	
• Unworthy or dirty	
• Like she wants to make him into the person she really needs	
"No different than before"	**5%**

Note: The top line of each section shows the percentage of girls who chose one or more of the answers in that section. Percentages do not total 100 percent because girls could choose more than one answer.

Though the data showed that many girls had positive feelings after having sex, *those same girls* said they would also feel "clingy, possessive, controlling, regretful, dirty, wanting to change the guy." In total, 85 percent of the girls said those negative feelings would arise. What it all adds up to is this: for a girl, sex changes *everything*.

Read the following paragraph carefully. In it we try to say all in one place what we discovered about girls and sex—stuff that most guys miss completely.

Girls view premarital sex very differently than guys do. Something changes emotionally for the average girl once she has sex with a guy. As one girl put it, "She knows that she has given a piece of herself to him—and she also knows he hasn't committed himself to her for a lifetime. They aren't married; he can leave whenever he gets tired of her." So now, whether the girl wants to or not, she begins to feel possessive and worried about losing him. She also feels that he now "owes" her something, such as spending a lot more time together. From that point on, even if she also has positive feelings, she still experiences strong feelings of possessiveness, insecurity, clinginess, or self-doubt.

Yikes! Not exactly what most guys expect when they accomplish what they believe is their greatest sexual achievement and… score.

Do you wonder how a physical act can change everything emotionally for a girl? Do you wish the positive feelings the girls talked about would outweigh their negative feelings? Do you think the hundreds of girls we interviewed were overreacting?

At the beginning of this book, we promised to take you inside

THE DAY AFTER...

the hearts and minds of the opposite sex, to show you things most guys never figure out about how girls are wired. Our purpose is to help you have happy, healthy relationships with the girls you know—or want to know. Even though some facts may be challenging, now you're hearing what girls really feel about this intriguing subject. Read on. Because there's a lot more.

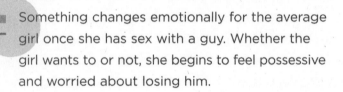

Something changes emotionally for the average girl once she has sex with a guy. Whether the girl wants to or not, she begins to feel possessive and worried about losing him.

What Girls Think About Sex

Do girls even *want* sex the way us hormone-insane guys do? You're probably saying, "Oh, please, please say they do." Okay.

Yes, sorta.

But also, definitely not.

To show you the facts that surfaced in our survey, we'll deliver five Sex Truths about girls. We're pretty sure you'll read this part. And if you don't quit when you hear something you don't like, you'll see by the end how it all comes together to be good news for both your long- *and* short-term future.

Let's start with something really basic—what *hot* means.

Sex Truth 1	What *hot* means to a girl

She doesn't think about sex as much as you do. And she doesn't dress to look hot because she wants to go to bed with you.

Guys think about sex only once every three seconds or so. That leaves one second for sports or pizza and one second for not thinking about anything at all. Actually, *think*—as a word to describe the male response to sex—is rarely accurate. It's more like being permanently hard-wired for distraction. Your brain chatter goes something like this: *I better get studying for—here she comes again—my geometry test... Oh, wow!... And my textbook is where?... I wonder what sex is going to be like… Oh, it's already time for lunch… I bet she wore that shirt because she wants some.* And on and on throughout the day.

We guys are so constantly distracted and motivated sexually that it simply doesn't occur to us that girls might be different. But they are. They're very different. Most girls, even the ones we think of as hot, go through their day without thinking about sex much at all. And when a girl wears "that shirt," it is not because she's saying, "Come and get it." In fact, what she wears has nothing to do with thoughts of sex at all. In case you doubt us, here's the proof. Read carefully:

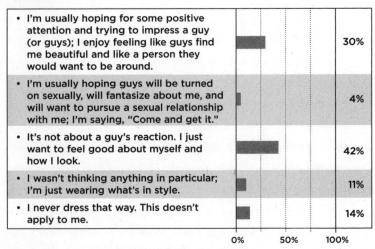

SURVEY	If you dress in form-fitting clothing that shows off your figure, what would most likely be going through your mind? (Choose one answer.)	
• I'm usually hoping for some positive attention and trying to impress a guy (or guys); I enjoy feeling like guys find me beautiful and like a person they would want to be around.		30%
• I'm usually hoping guys will be turned on sexually, will fantasize about me, and will want to pursue a sexual relationship with me; I'm saying, "Come and get it."		4%
• It's not about a guy's reaction. I just want to feel good about myself and how I look.		42%
• I wasn't thinking anything in particular; I'm just wearing what's in style.		11%
• I never dress that way. This doesn't apply to me.		14%

0%   50%   100%

Note: Due to rounding, the total slightly exceeds 100 percent.

Take a close look at those numbers. Only 4 percent of girls who dress in hot clothes are doing it to turn a guy on.

Since this discovery *really* did not compute, we asked the girls to explain. First, they explained a key point about how they are wired: when they see a hot guy, they can—and usually do—admire his looks without having a single thought of, *I want to go to bed with him.* Second, they admitted that they really don't get why we might be overwhelmed with "I want to go to bed with her" feelings when we see a hot girl who is dressed to show off her figure. (From now on, if anyone tells you that guys and girls are the same, take it as a politically correct piece of nonsense.)

In fact, after Shaunti and Lisa wrote *For Young Women Only,* which explains to girls how guys think, they found that almost every hot-dressing teenage girl they spoke with was horrified by the idea that a guy might be having sexual fantasies about her. The obvious question then is, "Why in the world are they dressing that way?"

The overwhelming majority of girls say they dress the way they do to get positive (but not sexual) attention. Mostly they just want to feel good about how they look.

One girl told us, "I want people to think, *That girl really tries to look nice and keep her body in shape.* I'm not trying to show off, at least not in a sexual way. I'm just trying to look and feel my best in the latest, hottest fashions."

Fact: 96 percent of the girls said they have no intention of tempting you to fantasize about sex with them—and most girls have absolutely no awareness of what images are racing around in your brain when you notice their tight-fitting clothes. They notice a guy's attention and conclude, *He thinks I'm cute,* never realizing that *cute* is probably the furthest thing from his mind.

When a girl wears "that shirt," it is not because she's saying, "Come and get it."

Sex Truth 2	How pressure works

When a guy pressures a girl for sex, her respect for him goes down.

We found that this truth is almost universal among girls, even among those who give in to the hard sell. Look at how cleverly we posed the question:

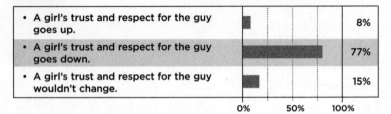

SURVEY	Do you think girls' respect and trust for a guy they are dating goes up or down if he starts vigorously pursuing a sexual relationship? (Choose one answer.)

• A girl's trust and respect for the guy goes up.	8%
• A girl's trust and respect for the guy goes down.	77%
• A girl's trust and respect for the guy wouldn't change.	15%

0%   50%   100%

Think about what this means. Suppose you and your girlfriend are just kissing. But thinking she wants more the same way you do, you decide to press just one more time, take things one step further, and—*wham!*—suddenly you and your chances for a good relationship with her really stink. Right when you thought she'd be so grateful for letting you take her on the pleasure trip of her life, you smell like yesterday's gym socks to her.

When we asked the girls to explain, they said things like this:

▸ "Even though I was all hormones that night, I was really disappointed that he let us get into sex. It ruined the trust thing."

▸ "If he led me into sex-type stuff this fast, he's probably led others the same way. And I don't want to think about how he's comparing me to other girls. It just messes things up."

Are you still clearheaded on the topic of what girls think about sex? We doubt it. But stay with us. What you learn will save you from all kinds of common mistakes and painful misunderstandings.

Sex Truth 3	How much she wants sex
Girls do have sexual desires. Compared to guys, her desires don't get triggered as easily. But once a girl is aroused, she can feel a strong desire for sex.	

Just when you thought there was no hope! Normal, healthy girls have normal, healthy sexual desires. The urge to merge that kicks in for guys at puberty powerfully affects girls as well. It's true. Look at what we asked on the survey:

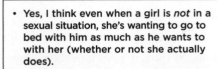

SURVEY Many people joke that teenage boys "only think about one thing." This question is designed to determine whether teenage girls think about and want that one thing as much as boys do. In your experience, if a girl and her boyfriend make out from time to time, but have *not* made the move to a sexual relationship, do you think the girl thinks about and physically wants sex with him as much as he probably does with her? (Choose one answer.)

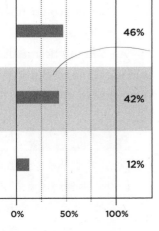

Yes, I think even when a girl is *not* in a sexual situation, she's wanting to go to bed with him as much as he wants to with her (whether or not she actually does).	46%
No, I think it's probably the guy that most wants the relationship to progress to actual sex. Most girls would be fine with continuing to make out without crossing that line.	42%
No, I think it's probably only the guy who wants the relationship to progress to actual sex, and she actively doesn't want to cross that line (even if she enjoys making out).	12%

Nearly half the girls surveyed believe they want sex as much as guys do, even when their hormones aren't being stirred up in a make-out situation. The rest of the girls said it was mostly or only the guy who wanted sex. And nearly all the girls said that once they *were* aroused, they would likely feel a physical desire to have sex.

So the reassurance here for guys is that girls aren't alien droids but are, in fact, sexually responsive beings. But the reassurance comes with a warning: girls respond differently. For example, as we said earlier, they don't get turned on by watching you walk by or thinking about you in a tight T-shirt. But once things have progressed to the point where they are actually turned on, most girls are just as tempted to cross the line as guys are.

Now, don't miss this: what most guys don't realize is that when a girl is really feeling tempted to have sex, what she wants most from the guy is not what most guys think.

We'll tell you what we discovered in a minute, but first we need to ask what happens to a girl emotionally when she does cross that line. Here's where we revisit the ugly truth we mentioned earlier.

Once things have progressed to the point where they are actually turned on, most girls are just as tempted to cross the line as guys are.

Sex Truth 4	What "free sex" costs
Outside of marriage, sex for a girl triggers powerful feelings of possessiveness, insecurity, clinginess, and self-doubt.	

While most girls identified some positive feelings after sex, even those girls and more—85 percent—listed surprisingly negative feelings. They chose words like *exposed, vulnerable, regretful, possessive, insecure, fear,* and *cheapened.* Whoa! Not good.

It isn't that girls think sex is somehow bad. Instead, to understand this, think back to that "Does he really like me?" insecurity we described in chapter 3. Sex ups the emotional stakes so much that, since she's not married to you, she suddenly starts worrying about losing you. And thinking about how to keep you.

What that means is that you can turn a carefree girl into someone you don't know—and probably don't want to know. She may still be a great girl, but now she's become possessive, clingy, controlling, and generally messed up. Raise your hand if that sounds fun.

Maybe the best single word we could use is *confused.* Without the security of marriage, a girl feels terribly confused after sex. And we have proof.

Did you notice in the chart on page 132 that many girls said they would feel more attachment after sex, but it would be in a "loving and free" way? We did. But then we checked the numbers…and, dude, those girls are crazy! Almost all (85 percent) of those who said they'd be "loving and free" also said they would feel possessive, worried, insecure, and clingy. That is *not* how most guys would define "loving and free."

Here's a real-life story to illustrate the crazy-confused point.

A girl we'll call Molly told us that she had signed an abstinence agreement with her parents and fully intended to save sex until mar-

riage. But then she had a pushy boyfriend and wasn't careful about the make-out situations she let herself get into. Eventually Molly went with her desires and began a sexual relationship with him.

Here's how she described her confused emotional state: "He's the only guy I've ever been with, so I need to marry him. He moved on and got another girlfriend, but I'm working my way back into his life. I have to."

Cue the creepy music.

Guys need to realize that Molly is not unusual. Girls all over the country struggle with these same powerful, unwanted feelings after they become sexually intimate. We're talking about scenarios of pain and confusion that most guys cause but don't know about, that most guys (you know it's true) *don't want to know about*. This problem may make for good teen-girl-angst movies, but it stinks in real life.

We guys want to convince ourselves that sex with a girl isn't that big a deal. We want it to be mostly "a physical thing" or "just having fun." But God didn't make humans to work that way. He wasn't joking when he told Adam and Eve that in sex "they will become one flesh." So if you still think unmarried sex is free and fun for all—no strings attached—it's time to leave the mall and live in the real world.

After Shaunti wrote a newspaper column about teenage sex, a girl e-mailed her this story:

> I was raised in a wonderful churchgoing home. But when I was fifteen, I began having sex. As a senior I found out that I had a sexually transmitted disease. I had no one to talk to. I was scared to death. But I continued to live my life disregarding consequences for a number of years.
>
> In college, I wanted to be "free." I prided myself on being "like a guy." As in, sleep with someone without any emotional restrictions. Let me say, with girls sex is always emotional. I turned to sex to cope with my low self-esteem. This was the ironic part. It was a vicious cycle. The more I slept around, the more insecure I would get. I used it to cope, and it made things worse.
>
> An interesting flip side is that nine times out of ten, guys get emotional too. They're just better at hiding it. It's hard for *anyone* to have sex and not get attached in some way or another.

"Nine times out of ten, guys get emotional too. It's hard for anyone to have sex and not get attached in some way or another."

Sex Truth 5	What she wants more than sex

A girl instinctively wants a guy to protect her and the relationship by not trying to have sex with her.

Girls told us that having a boyfriend who's strong enough not to pressure them for sex is their sincere desire. You see, girls instinctively realize that otherwise they'll have to deal with all those deep, negative emotions. And that means only one thing for you and the girl of your dreams: what she wants more than sex with you is for you to be man enough to protect her from it. Look carefully at this survey question, which sums it all up:

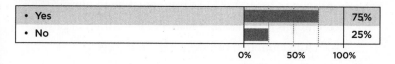

SURVEY	If you are in a make-out situation in a relationship that hasn't moved to sex, is something in you hoping that he will *not* try to go all the way?

• Yes	75%
• No	25%

0%   50%   100%

Even in a make-out situation, three out of four girls are hoping and wishing for one thing: that the guy will draw the line. As one girl put it, "I'm hoping he will be strong enough to protect me and the relationship and will absolutely *not* try to go all the way."

But what about those girls who said they physically wanted sex just as much as guys do? Is this true of them too? Yes. We cross-referenced the two questions and found that even two-thirds of *those* girls are still hoping their guy will be strong enough to back off!

One girl put it this way: "We've got hormones too, and it's not fair that the guy puts the pressure on the girl to be the one to stop things. Even though part of us wants it, we're hoping he'll be the leader and bring things to a halt." Another added, "To me, a guy who pushes for sex is showing the *opposite* of strength."

Not surprisingly, girls who had not already had sex were even more likely to hope that their boyfriend would not try to cross that line. But even among girls who had already had sex, six in ten were still hoping their boyfriend would be strong enough to draw the line.

So what happens in her heart when you make that tough choice to step back? We heard dozens of girls say that when a guy in a dating situation doesn't push for sex, a girl's trust and respect for him skyrocket. Here are just two examples:

- "As soon as I saw that Mike was not going to put me in a compromising situation, I relaxed. He went up hugely in my estimation; [he] became a hero in my eyes."
- "I really trust Richie because he never violated my standards. Now I can trust him with anything."

A DIFFERENT KIND OF HERO

Give It to Me One More Time

We've thrown a lot of numbers at you, and we've made some statements that you're probably still struggling to believe. So before we wrap up this chapter with some practical ideas for living smarter about sex, let's recap the five key truths our surveys uncovered (see facing page). These aren't the ideas about sex that hit you in the face when you turn on the television or go to the movies, are they? But they're exactly the truths that the girls you know and care about would tell you if they could.

Going to War to Protect Yourself—and Her

Temptations are thrown at us every day of our lives. Every day feels like a battle between what we know is right and what we're tempted to believe and do. And it's all too easy for guys to get trapped into believing things that are not only wrong but also dangerous.

So what can you do not only to defend yourself but also to protect the girls God brings into your life?

Fight the lies.

Ever made a list of the most common misconceptions about sex you hear? They are really just a pack of lies that can ensnare you if you don't identify them for what they are. Here are a few:

- Everyone's doing it. It's unrealistic to wait for sex until you're married.

Topic	Most guys think...	But the truth is...
Sex Truth 1. What *hot* means to a girl	*She dresses hot 'cause she wants me to have sex with her.*	She dresses hot to feel attractive and okay about herself.
Sex Truth 2. How pressure works	*She doesn't mind if I pressure her for sex, and she will think I'm more of a man if I do.*	If you pressure her for sex, her respect for you will go down.
Sex Truth 3. How much she wants sex	*She wants it as much as I do.*	She has hormones too, but she desires sex strongly only after she's aroused.
Sex Truth 4. What "free sex" costs	*If we have sex, she'll be fine. We'll be closer, but nothing else will change. If she says or implies "no strings attached," then that's how it will be.*	If she has sex with you, what she expects of you will change radically—and (for you) negatively—whether she wants it to or not.
Sex Truth 5. What she wants more than sex	*She secretly hopes I'll convince her— or arouse her enough—to have sex with me.*	She secretly hopes you'll protect her from having sex (even if she wants it too) because she knows that, for a girl, sex comes with powerful emotional strings attached.

▸ There's no reason to wait. *Carpe diem,* dude!

▸ There aren't any cute girls out there who care about waiting anyway. They're all giving in. So why don't I?

▸ Hey, I can cross lines without going all the way. I won't get burned.

▸ I want to be a real man. And real men have sex.

▸ I already did it. Might as well keep going.

▸ I'm sick of being the only one who hasn't done it.

The most dangerous of these lies contain a germ of truth that covers a deadly whopper. Take a look at any one of the thoughts on our list, and you can find the lie. For example:

▸ There really are reasons to wait—highly motivating ones that have paid off big-time for a lot of people. And if you've already done it, those reasons still exist. You can still do the right thing from now on.

▸ Having sex doesn't make you a man. (Who do you think you are—just one silly gland?)

▸ You aren't the only one who hasn't done it. And even if you are in the minority, it means you're the strongest man standing—the one who has fought the best fight, the one who cares the most about himself, his girl, and his future.

We've found that when lies about sex crowd in, it's helpful to actually speak God's truths over our life. Yes, we mean boldly say them out loud. That way the truth goes into your ears, pushes out the lies you might otherwise believe, and prepares you for the battle.

Those painted warriors charging down the hill with Mel Gibson in *Braveheart* weren't whispering, were they?

And here are some truths worth shouting:

> ‣ *There is no temptation too great for me. God always provides an escape route.* (See God's promise of this in 1 Corinthians 10:13.)
>
> ‣ *I have a future, a hope, and a high calling. So I'm not going to compromise!* (See Jeremiah 29:11.)

There really are reasons to wait—highly motivating ones that have paid off big-time for a lot of people.

Enlist support.

We've found that to stand firm against temptation, it's extremely helpful—almost essential—to enlist advice and encouragement from those who've fought the battles before us. Your parents may be great sources of counsel for you, or perhaps you can talk to a youth leader about what works…and what really doesn't. We've run across many teen guys who've formed accountability partnerships with a buddy. The key is, don't try to stand alone.

Recognize the consequences for you, not just for her.

As you surely know, the girl isn't the only one who will feel emotional consequences from sex outside a marriage commitment. In

Shaunti and Lisa's survey for the book *For Young Women Only,* they found that two-thirds of the guys admitted that when a relationship turned sexual, they began to wonder whether they could totally trust their girlfriend. And of course that messes everything up, *in addition to* the complications we talked about in this chapter.

Also, realize that sex before marriage can fill your head with lies that can come back to sabotage your relationship with the wife God brings you. Think about it. You know that you carry around a file of visual memories that never quite go away. Under the inevitable stresses of marriage, your brain will tell you that the sex you had before marriage was way better than anything you have with your wife. Of course, your brain is comparing reality with fantasy.

Trust us on this one: you don't want to have to deal with that kind of junk in your future. Instead, "pay it forward"—to your own marriage. Once you're married, you won't for one second regret all that effort you invested in waiting.

Stay out of harm's way.

It is a whole lot easier never starting something than trying to stop something once it's started. We don't need to go into detail here, do we? You know what we're talking about. Keep your hands to yourself, stay off those Web sites you know will melt your brain, and the temptations will be a lot easier to manage.

My (Eric's) wife spoke to a Seattle youth group where they had a panel of teen guys answering the girls' questions. One girl asked, "Where do you draw the line?" Then one of the guys on the panel grinned, gestured with his hands in front his body, and said, "Here's my rule: if I don't got it, I don't touch it!"

One guy said, "Here's my rule: if I don't got it, I don't touch it!"

Do a Joseph.

Despite all your good intentions, what will you do if you find yourself in a heated situation? Do a Joseph!

In a story in the book of Genesis, Joseph was a young man working for a powerful leader in Egypt, and his boss's wife was constantly asking him to sleep with her. What did he do? Did he enjoy the "harmless" flirting? No, he avoided her and told her, "No way!" every time. He feared disappointing God, and he knew he couldn't trust himself if he allowed himself to interact with her at all. Then came the day when she physically grabbed him. He tore out of her grasp and ran. He knew he couldn't stay in that tempting situation one more second.

You can "do a Joseph." No matter how far down the road you've gotten, whether you've crossed the line before or you haven't, just get up and run.

Score One for Manhood

We hope you've discovered some facts about girls and sex that are already changing the choices you'll make in the future—and all for the good. In a way, every guy is meant to score with girls. It's just that, as you've found out, what it really means to score is different from what most guys think. You thought it meant angling to get a girl to say yes to sex. Now you know the truth: girls see a sexually pushy guy as weak, not strong. They see a guy who is strong enough to hold the line as someone to admire and respect. And they deeply *want* you to protect both of you.

> A real man scores when he takes a stand for the best.

Bottom line, a real man scores when he takes a stand for the best—for himself and for the girl he's with—even if he has to stand alone. That's how he wins, now and in the future. You can know that every tough stand you take and every good decision you make will pay you back many times over. Sure, you'll live with a billion hormones pulsing through your body (just like the guys who are already sleeping around, by the way). But you'll live with a clear conscience, a lot of girls who appreciate, respect, and admire you—and no regrets.

We'll be praying for you. You *can* do this. One day you'll look back and see that, through all the temptations and tough choices, you chose to be a man.

THE GUY EVERY GIRL
WANTS...REALLY

*Could it be that the real
you is the real prize?*

(Eric) remember a recurring daydream I had as a junior-high kid growing up in Texas. In my dream there was a cute girl, a big problem, and a hero. I was the hero. (Well, what did you expect?) The daydream went like this:

Not far from our house, there was a small lake where I spent nearly every summer day. I'd imagine arriving at the lake to find a girl my age drowning. Even from the dock I could tell that the girl was beautiful. Awesome! So I'd dive in and save her life. That meant I had to wrap my arms around her, pull her to shore, then carry her up on the beach and administer first aid. Mouth-to-mouth resuscitation, of course.

Upon reviving, she immediately fell in love with me. In fact, in no time at all she simply could not keep her hands off me. Oh man, how I loved that dream!

But here's what Jeff and I want to tell you about such dreams: there's so much God-blessed truth in them. Seriously.

First of all, girls—all of them—want to be rescued in important ways. We hope you picked up on that amazing fact in the chapters you just read. Girls are looking for guys who bring confidence, character, fun, and good decisions to a relationship. They want to be saved, for example, from spending oh-so-dull hours alone. More important, they want to be rescued from painful insecurities—the fears that they're not pretty, not special, not okay. And even more important still, they want to be protected from dangers every girl must face, protected even from their own weakness.

Second, guys are born to be heroes. If this truth includes *us* (and—no kidding—it does), then it certainly includes *you*. God created ordinary guys to be extraordinary heroes to someone. And soon, if not already, that someone is likely to include a girl you think is very cute. What's more, God not only created us guys to want to be heroes, but he also stacked the deck in our favor so that we could succeed at that grand undertaking. Think about it:

1. You want to be confident, strong, fun, and smart.
2. She wants you to be all that too.
3. God created her to inspire you to become that.
4. God created her to see those qualities in you even before you do.

Okay, maybe we lost you on that last one. And that's why, one last time, we're going to do what we do best in *FYMO*, which is to hand over the surprising data.

> God created ordinary guys to be extraordinary heroes to someone.

"Tell Him This One Thing..."

At the end of the survey, we asked the girls what they most wanted to tell guys, and we gave them enough space to write whatever they wanted in response. Here's exactly what we asked: "Many guys look confident but are uncertain of themselves, especially when it comes to girls. If you could give these guys one piece of advice—advice about how to think about girls and themselves—what would it be?"

While we didn't know how the girls would answer, we hoped they would once again shatter what most guys would guess. They didn't disappoint. By far, the top response was a version of this very big idea, captured by one of many girls on the survey:

> **"You don't have to be perfect—just be yourself.**
> **That is the best person you can be."**

Of the hundreds of survey takers, not one girl wanted to tell a guy to improve his physical appearance or buy a girl nice things. Not one said she secretly wanted the cocky bad boy with the perfect schmoozy approach to girls. Instead, they overwhelmingly told the guys to relax and realize that girls don't expect perfection. They wanted guys to know that they don't have to put so much pressure on themselves. They wanted guys to believe in themselves, *be* themselves, and trust that their genuineness will carry them far. One girl summed it up perfectly:

> A lot of girls feel uncertain sometimes too. If you hold your head up and have a posture of confidence, you will begin to feel confident. In my opinion, the worst you can hear is no. So don't be afraid to approach a girl, because almost always she will appreciate the effort and it will make her day.

And that was just one of the many amazing comments we read. We've posted hundreds more responses from the girls on our Web site. You'll also find real girls on video, talking right to you. But in the meantime, here's a convincing sample of what they wanted to tell you:

- "A girl wants you for who you are, not for who you are pretending to be."
- "As lame as it sounds, just be yourself. You don't have to do anything stupid to impress her."
- "Girls appreciate it when you have the courage to tell them how you feel."

▸ "Even if you are afraid to talk to a girl you like, walk up and talk to her. It is really attractive and flattering to her when you risk your pride to do that."

▸ "Girls like a guy who is genuine. If you're trying to be something you're not, girls will see right through that."

▸ "Guys, just plainly be yourself. Girls love it when guys like to be themselves. If you are naturally funny, be funny. If you are serious, then just be serious. If you try to be something that you are not, that is a great big turnoff."

▸ "I've never been upset about being pursued, even when I turn a guy down. It is always flattering. Take a chance. It's a turnon."

▸ "Just be yourself and don't worry about rejection. Everyone gets rejected by someone at some point in life, and if you don't take that chance, then you might never know what could have been."

▸ "Don't be worried about your flaws, because girls have flaws too. Don't be someone you're not. Just be yourself."

▸ "If you are genuinely interested in getting to know a girl, let her know. If she is a kind and decent person, your attention will make her feel good. If she is unresponsive, thank goodness you saved yourself some time!"

▸ "There will always be a girl out there who will love you the way you are. So even if you get turned down, you shouldn't doubt yourself."

▸ "Just be yourself, because that way the girl who will get interested in you is going to fall for the real you."

We hope that you are as encouraged by these comments as we were. Girls—the same ones you'd want to hang out with—really do want you to be you. And they are much more forgiving and understanding of your flaws than most guys ever imagine.

Girls overwhelmingly told the guys to relax and realize that girls don't expect perfection.

The One Who Knows Your Future

Your future is bright. How can we say that? Well, actually, we didn't—God did. Jeremiah 29:11 tells us this: " 'I know the plans I have for you,' declares the LORD, 'plans to prosper you and not to harm you, plans to give you hope and a future.' "

According to the One who knows your future, what you have to look forward to is a "hope and a future." How much better can it get?

No doubt, these years of figuring out who you are as a man, what you want out of life, and what you want in a girl can be stressful. And all those male hormones don't help. But while the teen years are tough for guys, they're also the best opportunity you'll ever have to make the kinds of choices that will launch you toward a life of no regrets—the kind of life you deserve.

Do you see now that, for the best girl for you, the real you *is* the real prize? It's true. You're the hero she is waiting for.

We believe that what you've learned in these pages will set you apart from many guys who don't care enough—or respect the opposite sex enough—to make the effort to wise up. Even without any more deep thought about it, what you've discovered can still boost your confidence and open up new possibilities for your future. It just makes sense: a better understanding of girls will naturally lead to more rewarding friendships with them, which will lead to healthier dating relationships, which will in time lead to a strong, fulfilling marriage (*Ahem,* that includes a great sex life!) and a happy family.

But here we go one last time: don't just believe us; believe the girls. We leave you with this last piece of advice from one anonymous girl who took our survey:

> I have something that I want to say to the nice guys out there. Please, just be yourself. Don't try to be a bad boy, a player, or whatever. Or if you like to look a certain way but people put you down as geeky for liking that, who cares? A girl who really loves you won't care...or might even think you're cute for it.
>
> And finally, don't be afraid to wait. Who cares if you don't have a girlfriend by a certain year in school? Maybe God's got the right one waiting for you! Don't be so quick

to want to…umm…do it. Most girls aren't looking for that.

This is a sucky and awkward age, but don't let yourself feel too awkward around girls. Treat us with respect, start nice conversations with us, and see what happens. If the answer's no, then it's just not meant to be…but your girl is coming. Just wait!

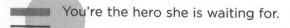 You're the hero she is waiting for.

Acknowledgments

During our eighteen months of research and writing, hundreds of people chipped in with invaluable insight, skill, advice, challenge, encouragement, and prayer. Space prevents individual shout-outs, but please know how much you are appreciated.

To the hundreds of young women who shared their perspectives in focus groups, interviews, and surveys: we promised you anonymity, but you know who you are, and we thank you. Your candor will give countless guys hope.

This book would be something quite different if it hadn't passed through the skillful hands of our editor, Dave Kopp, who managed to shape a manuscript with multiple authors into one consistent voice. Thank you, Dave, for your friendship and encouragement along the journey. Thanks also to Eric Stanford for your careful edits.

Once again, the professional survey that anchors this book was skillfully guided by Chuck Cowan of Analytic Focus (www.analytic focus.com) and conducted by the team at Decision Analyst (www .decisonanalyst.com), including the amazing help of Vicki Keathley. We're so grateful for our partnership with you over the years.

For every person who turns a page in this book and laughs out loud at a cartoon, know that the cartoons are the product of Don Patton's creative mind and skillful pencil. Thanks, Don. We only wish we could've created this book entirely in comic book format.

Finally, we want to thank the kids who walked this road with us: the two littlest Feldhahns, who will someday be teenagers aptly navigating those challenging years, and the always insightful Rice teens, who gave us fun stories and made sure the book had at least a little coolness to it. You guys rock.

conversation guide

CONVERSATION GUIDE

Chapter 1: What Most Guys Never Know

Recap

Think of *FYMO* as a manual to help you understand the most frustrating—and yet most fascinating—subject you know: the girls in your life. Unlike many advice books, this one uses solid research to tell you what girls themselves think about some of the topics that mystify you most. It will give you confidence as you relate to girls you like…and especially to that *one* girl you *really* like.

Questions

1. Rate yourself on how cool you act around girls, using a scale from 1 ("I'm always embarrassing myself") to 10 ("Chicks are sooo into me"). If you're working through this conversation guide in a group, have one of the other guys rate you using that same scale. When do you feel most awkward around girls?

2. What are you hoping to get out of reading and discussing *FYMO*?

3. You might have read books by youth pastors or Christian writers telling teens how to do relationships. What do you think you can learn from this book that's different?

4. Jeff and Eric say, "We challenge you to use these powers [of understanding girls] wisely and not for your own selfish purposes." What are some "selfish purposes"? What are some positive ways to use this information?

5. Read Genesis 1:27. What does this verse say to you about the dignity that God intended both guys and girls to have?

Real-Life Challenge

Pick one girl friend (not girlfriend) you trust, and see if she would be willing to let you ask her for her "girl perspective" from time to time as you work through *FYMO*. She'll be a great resource when you find yourself baffled by females.

Note: with each real-life challenge, report back next time on how it went.

Chapter 2: Abercrombie Boy vs. Our Hero, Average Joe

Recap

There's a contest going on out there between guys who look like models...and the rest of us. Who's going to get the girl? Surprisingly, it could be Average Joe. That's because, as weird as it sounds, looks aren't as important to girls. They're more attracted by inner qualities like a sense of humor, thoughtfulness, fun, self-confidence, and faith. And those are qualities Average Joe can acquire.

Questions

1. Jeff missed a chance with a girl because he didn't believe she would want to keep going out with him. How about you? If you see a girl you like, are you more likely to assume that she *will* be interested in you or that she *won't* be? Why?

2. Jeff and Eric claim that girls are more interested in inner qualities than in outward looks. Does that match up with your observation of how girls react to guys—or not? Give an example that supports your answer.

3. Check out 1 Samuel 16:7. How is the way girls evaluate others maybe more like the way God evaluates people?

4. Name a guy lots of girls like as a friend or boyfriend. What inner qualities does he have that you think attract girls to him? What can you learn from his example?

5. On a scale from 1 ("I stink at it") to 5 ("I could give lessons"), how would you rate yourself in these areas?

sense of humor	1	2	3	4	5
thoughtfulness	1	2	3	4	5
fun	1	2	3	4	5
self-confidence	1	2	3	4	5
faith	1	2	3	4	5

What would it take for you to climb up to a 4 or a 5 in each quality?

Real-Life Challenge

Choose one area from the previous question that you are weak in, then do something to start changing your reputation in that area. (For example, if you're not exactly the king of good times, plan something fun for a group of your guy and girl friends to do together.)

Chapter 3: Why Good Girls Like Bad Boys

Recap

One of the most frustrating things about girls is their tendency to fall for guys we know are jerks. What's up with that? Turns out, girls aren't attracted so much to what makes the bad boys bad. Instead, they appreciate the *positive* qualities that bad boys display—positive qualities like self-confidence. If good guys will learn some lessons from bad boys, the girls will go for the good guys more often.

Questions

1. What are the "bad boys" at your school like? How do they treat girls? How do girls respond?

2. The authors say, "Girls are overwhelmingly attracted to bad boys because of their positive qualities." What are some positive qualities you've seen in bad boys?

3. According to this chapter, girls respond to bad boys' attention because bad boys often give the best answer to the girl's secret question *(Am I lovable? Am I attractive?)*. Did

you realize that girls were secretly asking that question and secretly insecure? How can you use that knowledge to become a better friend or boyfriend?

4. Do you struggle with feeling insecure around girls? What causes your insecurity? What can you do to shore it up?

5. When Joshua was chosen to lead Israel, what did God keep telling him? For the answer, read Joshua 1:6–9. In your interactions with girls, where is God calling you to be "strong and courageous"?

6. What helps you have more confidence around girls? How can you help them feel more confident about *themselves*?

Real-Life Challenge

Find a place where you can listen in on conversations that bad boys are having with girls. What good can you learn from it that you could apply in a positive, God-honoring way?

Chapter 4: When Girls Stop Making Sense

Recap

Sometimes the way girls act seems so random. But maybe it isn't, say Jeff and Eric. The fact is, something is usually going on inside a girl or in her world that is driving the behavior. And that's not the time for a guy to give up on understanding her. Instead, that's when he can try to figure out what's going on beneath the confusing surface. There's a reason in there, and you can crack the code!

Questions

1. Give an example of baffling girl behavior you've encountered. How did you react to that kind of confusing behavior?

2. Why do you think God made males and females so different that they have to work hard to understand each other?

3. Eric and Jeff identify four reasons for the apparent randomness of girl behavior: (a) something you've done, even if you don't realize you did it, (b) something about her circumstances (it's not about you), (c) something that's going on inside her, and (d) hormone poisoning. Give an example of a time when you discovered that one of these reasons accounted for the behavior of a girl you know.

4. Read 1 Peter 3:7. What does this verse suggest about a guy's responsibility to make an extra effort to understand and help girls?

5. Imagine that a girl you like seems down today. What are a couple ways to start a conversation with her that would gently invite her to share what she's thinking? What are a couple things *not* to say?

Real-Life Challenge

The next time a girl in your life does something that makes no sense to you, practice looking for the reason, like trying to pick up on her nonverbal signals and asking her friendly questions to find out what's happening inside her or in her world.

Chapter 5: Breaking Up, Breaking You

Recap

So often a guy thinks his girl is totally into him—right up to the point where she tosses him into the Dumpster. Are girls cruel, or are guys dumb? Neither one. It's just that girls have a different way of handling it when their feelings about a guy start cooling off. They give out subtle signals that we barely pick up on. Unless, of course, we've read this chapter and learned what to look for and what to do before it's too late.

Questions

1. Has a girlfriend ever broken up with you? How did she do it? Were you surprised? (No pressure to share this stuff with your group if you don't want to.)

2. Have you ever felt that girls secretly take pleasure in breaking a guy's heart? After reading this chapter, did you change your mind about that? If so, in what way?

3. If you've ever been dumped by a girl, think back to that situation. What signals—that you missed—was she sending out to say she wasn't happy in the relationship anymore?

4. Read Luke 8:18. Okay, we realize that we're taking and applying this verse out of context. But still, it's true that if a guy who's in a relationship with a girl isn't alert, "what he thinks he has will be taken from him." So then what might it mean for you to "consider carefully how you listen" to your girl?

5. How do you know when a relationship is worth fighting for versus when it's time to move on?

Real-Life Challenge

If you're in a boyfriend-girlfriend relationship right now, the next time you're just walking somewhere or driving around together, check to see how she's feeling about things and give her an open-ended chance to share. For example, "I love hanging out with you, but I know sometimes I probably can drive you nuts without meaning to. Is there anything you've been wanting to talk to me about?"

Chapter 6: No Dropped Calls

Recap

One part of your brain understands that she's just another humanoid. Another part of your brain detects her presence, then immediately shuts down, paralyzing your vocal powers in the process. How is a poor teen guy supposed to carry on a conversation with a girl, particularly one he likes, without looking like a loser? Here's the weird thing: conversation is more about listening than talking.

Questions

1. Think about a time you said something stupid—or couldn't say anything at all—in the presence of a girl you liked. If you're in a group, tell about it—but first make a pact that none of the stories go beyond the group.

2. This chapter is mostly about listening. Why do you think listening matters so much to girls? What tips about listening (relax, ask good questions, and so on) did you find most helpful? Why?

3. If you were to ask the girls in your life to give you a grade on how well you listen, what do you think it would be? Why?

4. Read Proverbs 18:13. Why is being too quick to talk considered folly and shame?

5. What can you say differently, or how can you improve what you say, when talking with girls?

Real-Life Challenge

This week, when you're having a conversation with a girl, practice asking good questions and getting her to talk about herself. Note how she responds.

Chapter 7: What It Really Means to Score

Recap

Guys talk about it…a lot. Not that you always *believe* them. We're talking about "scoring" with girls here. Now remember, girls don't take sex as lightly as guys seem to. In fact, girls report that having sex with a guy tends to make them insecure and possessive. Not only that, but they also report that what they really want is for a guy to protect them from going too far in their physical relationship.

Questions

1. Did you start reading the book with this chapter? Be honest!

2. According to current research, having sex before marriage changes a relationship—for the worse. Have you heard guys complain about their girls becoming clingy after the relationship got sexual? What did they say? (No names, please.)

3. This chapter makes some amazing claims. For example...

   ‣ Most girls don't know they're getting guys sexually heated up when they dress hot.

   ‣ Most girls lose respect for guys who try to get them into bed.

   ‣ Most girls want the guy to take the lead in seeing that the relationship doesn't cross the line.

   What part of this chapter was most surprising to you? Why?

4. Which pieces of advice about not crossing the line (fight the lies, enlist support, recognize the consequences, and so on) do you think are most helpful? Why? Got any other tips for staying strong to share with your conversation group?

5. If a guy has already had sex, how (if at all) does that change the way he should try to be responsible in his guy-girl relationships?

6. Look up Titus 2:6. When it comes to sex, is self-control something you can learn? If so, how?

Real-Life Challenge

If you're dating a girl and the two of you have *not* had sex, reassure her that you're not going to pressure her for it. If you *have* had sex, talk about how to put your relationship back on a more God-honoring track.

Chapter 8: The Guy Every Girl Wants...Really

The Recap

Guys are born to be heroes—to rescue and protect—and girls want them to be just that way. But that doesn't mean you have to pretend to be something you're not. In fact, girls overwhelmingly reported that they want guys to just be themselves. And as you work to become the best *you* you can be, God will lead you into the wonderful future he has for you—with a great girl by your side. Believe it!

Questions

1. This chapter claims, "God created ordinary guys to be extraordinary heroes to someone." Have you ever done anything heroic—even something small—to rescue or protect a girl? If so, tell about it.

2. Read John 3:20–21. What do the concepts of coming into the light and living by the truth suggest about how you can be genuine around girls—and around everyone else for that matter?

3. As you look ahead to the rest of your dating years and to marriage, what kind of a man do you dream of becoming? List four or five traits.

4. As you think back over the book as a whole, what insight sticks with you the most? Why that one?

5. How will the way you treat girls be different as a result of having read this book? How will you change as a friend? as a boyfriend? as a Christian brother?

WANT MORE?

>>

for young men only

Visit www.foryoungmenonly.com for lots of additional information including:

- Access the entire survey
- Read hundreds of comments from the girls surveyed
- Watch video clips of the girls "talking straight" to guys
- View the *For Young Men Only* music video
- Interact in online forums where you and the teenage girl readers of *For Young Women Only* can ask and answer questions
- Download a guide for youth leaders with suggestions for creating *For Young Men Only* and *For Young Women Only* small groups

why are guys
So Weird?

from the author of the bestselling *for women only*

shaunti feldhahn
and lisa a. rice

for young
women only

what you
need to know
about how
guys think

Guys will be guys. And now girls can know what
that means! *For Young Women Only* dives into the
mysterious inner-workings of the teenage male
mind so that you can begin to understand why
guys say and do what they do.

SURPRISING TRUTHS TO IMPROVE
EVERY SIGNIFICANT RELATIONSHIP

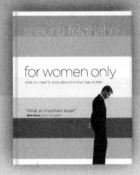

For Women Only is full of eye-opening revelations you need to not only understand the man in your life, but to support and love him in the way he needs to be loved.

Take the guesswork out of trying to please your wife or girlfriend and begin loving her in the way she needs. Easily. *For Men Only* is a straightforward map that will lead you straight into her heart.

Discover first-hand about the longings that drive your kids' seemingly illogical decisions, the truth behind those exasperating "attitude problems," and what your children would tell you if they could trust you to truly listen.

About the Authors

JEFF FELDHAHN is an attorney and the owner of the tech company World2One. With his wife, Shaunti, he wrote the best-selling *For Men Only*.

ERIC RICE is the owner, director, and producer of 44 Films. Eric lives in Atlanta area with his wife, Lisa, and their four teenage children.

SHAUNTI FELDHAHN is a nationally syndicated newspaper columnist, public speaker, and best-selling author whose books include *For Women Only*, *For Young Women Only* (with Lisa Rice), and *For Parents Only*.